Shelley's Myth of Metaphor

Shelley's
Myth of Metaphor

JOHN W. WRIGHT

UNIVERSITY OF GEORGIA PRESS

To Susan

The Vegetative Universe opens
    like a flower from the Earth's center
In which is Eternity. It expands
    in stars to the Mundane Shell
And there it meets Eternity again,
    both within and without,
And the abstract Voids between
    the stars are the Satanic Wheels.

William Blake,
Jerusalem I, 13:34-37

I

SHELLEY'S *A Defence of Poetry,* unlike most of its counterparts in the long contest between science and poetry, contains a highly original and philosophically significant answer to the question of how the poet and poetry provide that knowledge upon which instruction and delight can be said finally to depend. The force of the theory of experience upon which he based the *Defence* long went unnoticed and could, of course, have been only a mildly interesting subject as long as it was assumed that philosophically he offered only a poet's variation on the metaphysically bankrupt themes of platonic transcendentalism. And until recently this has been the prevailing opinion about the basic principles of the *Defence* and about Shelley's later poetry generally. But recent studies of Shelley have begun to estimate more accurately his relationship and debt to eighteenth-century British philosophy, and their results suggest, as it is hoped this study will, that Shelley regarded certain aspects of the empirical philosophy as necessary if not sufficient conditions for all speculation about experience. Instead of being an inspired scrapbook of platonic rhetoric, the *Defence* is more nearly an inspired synthesis of conformable elements of empiricism and platonism.

By emphasizing the role imagination plays in the formation as well as in the expression or representation of human experience (a philosophic premise which follows easily from principles which rule any synthetic or generative agency out of nature), and by recognizing an important relationship between the synthetic power of imagination and the synthetic function of metaphor, Shelley was able to develop extensively the analogy between the way the mind makes and modifies the world it takes for reality and the way a poet makes a poem and modifies the world of human culture. The philosophic center of his argument in the *Defence* consists of his insights into the nature of the materials and the dynamics of this process of composition, which I shall call a composition theory of experience. This theory and the coherence theory of truth which accompanies it indicate, for example, why he regarded the poet's activity not merely as a special kind of linguistic or imaginative behavior, but as the paradigmatic form of all human mental activity. His procedure was not simply a rhetorical generalization along platonic lines of the idea of *poesis,* but a philosophically informed application of the principle that "all things exist as they are perceived, at least in relation to the percipient,"[1] to the problem of knowledge in all forms of human culture. Part of his position, as his other prose amply demonstrates, was found ready-made in the principles and implications of British empirical philosophy; part of it came from his insight into correspondences between platonic and empirical ideas about the structure of experience; and part, probably the most important and novel element, came from his insight into the nature of metaphor and its role in the formation of experience, thought, and culture. These points will be considered further in the course of this essay, but it will be useful to indicate more fully

---

[1] *The Complete Works of Percy Bysshe Shelley,* ed. R. Ingpen and W.E. Peck (London, 1965), VII, p. 137. All subsequent references to the works of Shelley will be to this edition unless otherwise indicated, and where practicable will be interpolated into the text. The following abbreviations of titles of frequently-cited prose works will be used: *A Defence of Poetry: D; On Life: OL; Speculations on Metaphysics: SM.* A convenient account of the background and circumstances of the composition and publication of *A Defence of Poetry* is available in the editor's Introduction in *A Defence of Poetry and The Four Ages of Poetry,* ed. John E. Jordan (New York, 1965), pp. vii-xxxi.

here the nature of approaches made already to this side of Shelley's thought and then, in greater detail, the character of his synthesis of received opinion.

C.E. Pulos has studied the importance of traditional skepticism and eighteenth-century British philosophy in the formation of Shelley's later thought in *The Deep Truth.* Unfortunately he makes only three passing references to *A Defence of Poetry* and misses the evidences it offers of Shelley's synthesis of empiricism and platonism, skepticism and idealism. He observes, "the central conflict in Shelley's philosophy is that between his empiricism and his platonism. The poet's resolution could have been suggested only by a philosopher who had dealt with the same problem."[2] His argument rejects Berkeley as a significant agent in the reformation of Shelley's thought in favor of Sir William Drummond and, vaguely, the "positive issues of skepticism—probability and faith" as "implied" in Drummond's *Academical Questions.*[3] Actually Drummond does only hint at this theme of a reconciliation. In his Preface Shelley had read: "I think it may not be improper to observe here, that although I have generally understood the word *idea* in the same sense with most other modern philosophers, I am yet ready to acknowledge, that it may bear another and an higher meaning. I cannot, indeed, comprehend anything, which is neither a sensation, nor obtained from one: I do not, however, on that account, deny the existence of divine and intelligible ideas."[4] Shelley probably learned much more from other philosophers who dealt with the problem—from Berkeley's *Siris,* for example, or more probably from Coleridge's Essay VIII and Essay IX in Section the Second of the 1818 edition of *The Friend* and from *Biog-*

[2] *The Deep Truth* (Lincoln, 1954), p. 111.

[3] Ibid., p. 50. His interpretation of Shelley's sense of Plato's skepticism is very informative.

[4] *Academical Questions* (London, 1805), I, xiv.

raphia Literaria, Chapters V-XII, which he took with him to Italy.[5] Both works survey western philosophic traditions with an eye to reunion in philosophy, and in *The Friend* Coleridge treats directly the subject of a "reconcilement of the Platonic and Baconian methods."

In *The Apocalyptic Vision in the Poetry of Shelley* R.G. Woodman demonstrates well the distinctive features of Shelley's uses of platonism and moves closer than any other study has to discovering the empirical-platonic synthesis behind his vision of the world as a poem. Woodman writes, "The implication is clear: Shelley's apocalyptic vision (i.e., the vision of a universe continuously created as distinct from a universe continuously perceived) belongs within a verbal universe. . . . It is, like Plato's republic, a pattern set up in heaven."[6] Once Shelley's perception of congruence between empirical and platonic theories of experience is evident, it becomes clear that the "verbal universe" described by Woodman emerges as a heaven of *poesis* in a universe of poetry and, as I hope to show, that Shelley's apocalyptic vision develops and fulfills itself through a myth of metaphor.

Neglect of the special character of Shelley's philosophic background and his distinctive sense of the nature and role of language—particularly metaphor—in the evolution of human culture has frequently blighted studies of his poetry and criticism.[7] Even Earl Wasser-

[5] See note 17 below.

[6] *The Apocalyptic Vision in the Poetry of Shelley* (Toronto, 1954), p. 20.

[7] Cf. Carlos Baker, *Shelley's Major Poetry* (Columbia, 1959), for a now widely-known interpretation of Shelley as a platonist which takes almost no account of Shelley's understanding of empirical philosophy. Harold Bloom, in *Shelley's Mythmaking* (New Haven, 1959), largely ignores the *Defence, Adonais,* and the relations between them. More recently Earl J. Schulze has argued convincingly in *Shelley's Theory of Poetry: a Reappraisal* (The Hague, 1966), against the view of Shelley as an other-worldly platonist (spurred and bridled, as it seemed to

man, who has effectively analyzed these errors of interpretation and repudiated the fiction of Shelley as
naively platonist, nonetheless slides often, especially in
his studies of *Adonais* and the *Defence,* into arguments
and forms of expression which presuppose some of the
very assumptions his detailed interpretations clearly re-
fute. Since the present essay is much concerned with the
nature and direction of Shelley's creative synthesis of elements of apparently rival philosophic traditions, Wasserman's important treatment of closely-related
problems needs brief consideration at the start.

His studies consistently ascribe a species of transcendentalism to Shelley's poetry and poetics. The theoretical basis of this general position is developed in his
chapter on *Mont Blanc* in *The Subtler Language,* which
everywhere supposes that Shelley received a quasi-
systematic philosophy—an "ontology"—from a position he identifies as the "Intellectual Philosophy" or, alternately, the "intellectual system."[8] From this
assumption Wasserman's brilliant analysis of *Mont
Blanc* develops a quite credible account of how Shel-

some, by the utilitarian debacle of his early years), and has indicated that eighteenth-century British philosophy formed the basis of the "psychological empiricism" at the root of Shelley's
poetics. "It is tempting," Schulze observes, "to associate Shelley's thought with Berkeley's" (p. 63). The correctness of this association can be established by looking at what Shelley saw in
empiricist epistemology and how he adapted it to his own ends.
Schulze also finds that "Shelley's radical empiricism combines
in his philosophic thought with a radical humanism in which
'life and the world' take on the greatest possible human significance" (p. 69). In a review of Schulze's book in the *Michigan
Quarterly Review,* VII (1968), 219-221, Earl R. Wasserman objects to what he calls the "existentialist" bias of these empiricist
and humanist conclusions: "I can find no aspect of Schulze's
analysis that does not become fully intelligible in the context of
Shelley's assumption of a transhuman absolute that subsumes
the human" (p. 220). That this assumption is Wasserman's
rather than Shelley's is considered below.

[8] *The Subtler Language* (Baltimore, 1959), pp. 195-250.

ley's thought transcends the antinomies of nihilistic materialism and solipsistic idealism. The argument leads to the following conclusion:

> It must by now bw obvious that the summit of Mont Blanc is the symbol of Power. The transcending capacity of dream has granted insight into that transcendent Power, unknowable in normal experience or in terms of the idealistic definition of existence.[9]

The more general, philosophic form of this position concludes the essay:

> The thoughts we call "things" would be meaningless if thought did not have the imaginative power to float above the darkness of the universe, and, in dreams, bring to those "things" a knowledge of a supernal, immutable essence that is the ground and Power of everything.[10]

It is true that Shelley learned from Berkeley, Hume, and others the senses in which things may be thoughts and thoughts things. It is misleading, however, to claim that he conceived of imagination as a power which (eros-like) ascends (in dreams) to a supernatural experience of immutable essence and descends as poetry, and that he "obliquely hints" at this epistemology and ontology in *Mont Blanc*. The misapprehension is in one sense built into Wasserman's conception of "the paradoxical nature of the ontology *taught* by the Intellectual Philosophy" (italics mine).[11]

> According to this doctrine the known data of the mind and their unknowable outer causes dissolve into a higher unity which can be defined discursively only by

[9] Ibid., p. 231.
[10] Ibid., p. 240.
[11] Ibid., p. 236.

the double assertation that reality is that which is the source of our impressions and at the same time is those impressions aroused by an outer something. Neither definition is sufficient, for each independently is false; reality must be defined from both positions simultaneously. [12]

In effect, the Intellectual Philosophy taught Shelley an intuitive transcendentalism. This would not be true even if the Intellectual Philosophy were a received position rather than Shelley's phrase for a range of exciting speculations and approaches to speculation. As things stand, both the manner and fact of his association of the general position with Sir William Drummond's views and his own clear account of the method and result of that widely-diffused approach to philosophic analysis make it clear that the constitutive power of imagination is an idea he developed later and conceived in other than transcendentalist terms. [13] Wasserman cites only fragments of the following statement of the character of the intellectual system:

It establishes no new truth, it gives us no additional insight into our hidden nature, neither its action nor itself. Philosophy, impatient as it may be to build, has much work yet remaining, as pioneer for the overgrowth of ages. It makes one step towards this object; it destroys

[12] Ibid., p. 202.

[13] See Chapters III and IV below and Albert S. Gerard, *English Romantic Poetry* (Berkeley, 1968), p. 164 ff.: "What we find here is not only what M.H. Abrams has rightly called 'a combination of Platonism and psychological empiricism,' (*The Mirror and the Lamp: Romantic Theory and the Critical Tradition*, New York, p. 130): it is a deeply felt awareness that, while Platonism and psychological empiricism may be mutually exclusive, the creative power of the poet cannot be doubted." The present essay is a study of Shelley's thought on this theme: it might reasonably be said his doubts about the creative power of the poet are evident everywhere except in the *Defence*.

error and the root of error. It leaves, what it is too often the duty of the reformer in political and ethical questions to leave, a vacancy. It reduces the mind to that freedom in which it would have acted, but for the misuse of words and signs, the instruments of its own creation. (*OL,* VI, 195)

Like many other observations in his philosophic writings, this passage from the essay *On Life* tells us more about what Shelley recognized as frontier philosophy and the limits set on speculation by the great philosophic minds of the eighteenth century than it does about his own position on the way the world is. The reflections which follow it constitute neither ontology nor transcendentalism but a kind of phenomenalism in which Shelley's attention is directed to the subtle relations between belief and immediate experience and to the strangeness he encountered as one initiate "in" a world transformed by the awareness that "natural" distinctions between self and other, subject and object, idea and thing are but conventions received as elements of nature. The "vacancy" opened by the Intellectual Philosophy is the crux of the meditative phenomenological experiments built into the poetry of *Mont Blanc.* (Wasserman's account tends to convert this philosophic poem of meditation into a theological argument for the existence of a god.) Shelley offers no solution to the fascinated doubts in which the poem ends. Those same concerns still move, two years later, among the conceptual interstices which threaten the marriage of love and art in the mythopoeic cosmos of *Prometheus Unbound.*[14] They find a resolution only when he develops in the *Defence* an account of *how* imagination creates and recreates the universe of poetry.

From his supposition that the Intellectual

14 Wasserman's account of Shelley's myth-making is considered at the beginning of my Chapter IV.

Philosophy supplied Shelley with a way to transcendentalist ontology, Wasserman's argument leads to a search
throughout the major poetry for its consequences, and it
is the effect of this position in his accounts of the *Defence* and *Adonais* which is particularly relevant to the
present study. The assumption that Shelley's thought
and poetry answer to a transcendentalist principle is
formulated in "Shelley's Last Poetics": "although the
transcendent One is postulated in the structure of Shelley's reality, it is not, the commentators notwithstand-
ing, an operative factor in the poetics of the *Defence*." [15]
The second part of this statement is correct and important, but the first part treats one of the frames of reference of Shelley's thought as if it were the object of a
philosophic or religious commitment. It is everywhere
apparent that Shelley's vision of experience has cultural,
personal, and theoretical dimensions which constitute
one of the most nascent and open visions ever to inspire
great poetry, and we need to read his works and understand his thought without sacrificing the indeterminacy
which animated it and, as he thought, haunted him like
Actaeon's hounds.

Wasserman's valuable account of the logic of the
concepts of Shelley's poetics does provide a strikingly
effective synthesis or systematization of ideas which
went into the argument of the *Defence* from a tentative
and conjectural search for foundations of an aesthetic
epistemology. And he is able even to show how the theory of art expressed in the *Defence,* far from being an
irresponsible rhapsody, offers a viable basis for practical criticism. [16] But in all this his guiding concern is with
the elements of Shelley's *poetics* (in the conventional
sense) and with their intelligibility as "instruments of

[15] In *From Sensibility to Romanticism,* ed. F.W. Hilles and
Harold Bloom (New York, 1965), pp. 487-511.

[16] Ibid., pp. 508-511.

poetic analysis." Quite different questions guided Shelley's reflections on how poetry and the poet could and did possess the knowledge and experience to answer the opposition and establish the paramount importance of poetry in the evolution of society and the well-being of the individual person. Wasserman has observed that "there is then no inconsistency between Shelley's so-called 'Platonism' and an associational psychology [of aesthetic experience]; the two complemented each other to form a coherent system." This conclusion is generally true but it does not express strongly enough the conditions of Shelley's integration of two philosophic traditions, and it tends to read a purpose of systematic poetics into interests which had quite a different orientation. It is evident that Shelley wrote often (and in a variety of moods) of relations between transcendent power and individual existence, but it does not follow that we can argue from this theme to his belief in or systematic treatment of the ontology of transcendentalist participation as Wasserman does, for example, when he says of Shelley's criteria for aesthetic realization, "it is consistent with Shelley's [assumed] ontology that he can conceive of the poetic act indifferently either as a creation of ideal order or a kind of discovery of it; *because* the order created by the mind is the order that truly *subsists in reality* beneath the veil of appearance and mutability" (italics mine). [17] Relations and questions like these are the great issues explored in Shelley's earlier philosophic prose and into which he was initiated by what he called the "Intellectual Philosophy"; they are not the principles of a Shelleyan world-system or a systematic poetic.

In the *Defence* and elsewhere in his prose and poetry after 1815, Shelley used the traditional image of the circle as a metaphor for the field of experience and for rep-

[17] Ibid., p. 500.

resenting the structure and dynamics of the mind's imaginative activity. The relationships of center, circumference, and radiation provided by this figure illuminate important distinctions between the source, progress, and end of mental activity or experience. It is possible to indicate in a general way the kind of correspondence Shelley found between platonic and empirical philosophy by paraphrasing the statement attributed traditionally to Hermes Trismegistus: "God is that circle whose center is everywhere and whose circumference is nowhere."[18] For the empiricists who seem to have been important in the formation of Shelley's later philosophic opinions, Bishop Berkeley, David Hume, and Sir William Drummond, Trismegistus' statement about God would read: "experience is that circle whose center is everywhere where the mind is and whose circumference is nowhere." Here is Shelley's own variation on the phrase: "Poetry is indeed something divine. It is at once the center and circumference of all knowledge; it is that which comprehends all science and that to which all science must be referred" (*D*, VII, 135). It expresses with extraordinary precision, as we shall see, his synthesis of idealism and empiricism. His use of the image of a field for the activity of imagination is one of the basic principles of the *Defence*—it is that which comprehends all its platonism and that to which all its empiricism should be referred. From the point of view of its philosophic foundations the other basic principle of his argument is the idea that metaphor is a direct instru-

[18] Frances A. Yates, in her *Giordano Bruno and the Hermetic Tradition* (Chicago, 1964), p. 247, gives the *Liber XXIV philosophorum*, "a pseudo-Hermetic treatise of the twelfth century," as the source of this phrase. George Poulet, *Les Métamorphoses du Cèrcle* (Plon, 1961), p. iii, cites the same source and mentions Shelley in his account of the metamorphoses of the circle figure among the romantic authors, pp. 136-176. See also Marjorie H. Nicolson, *The Breaking of the Circle* (New York, 1960), p. 47 ff., and *The Subtler Language*, p. 203.

ment and form of human knowledge—it is the mode of apprehension and expression by which imagination creates experience. Shelley's treatment of these two principles (and much thought in the twentieth century has confirmed the value of his innovations) constitutes an aesthetic epistemology which is a significant rival to the philosophic ideas which then and afterwards supported empiricist and rationalist theories of experience. Shelley's position reunites the world and the mind, reincorporates science in art, and, finally, I believe, regards instruction and delight as one in the power of imagination to create experience. I call it a myth of metaphor because he regards the world for the mind as a value-determined composition of myth from the metaphors which imagination creates as the substance of immediate experience and the body of true poetry in all its forms in human culture.[19] To illuminate these principles and the nature of the myth they support I shall consider, first, Shelley's original view of metaphor in relation to the then generally-received opinion about language and knowledge, next his use of the circle and related figures to express the idea that experience is essentially the creation of myth from metaphor, and, finally, *Adonais* as an embodiment of the basic principles of the *Defence* and a confirmation of my interpretation of them.

[19] For its title phrase and several essential elements of its philosophic perspective my essay is deeply indebted to C.M. Turbayne's great and revolutionary book, *The Myth of Metaphor* (Yale, 1962), which will be reissued by the University of South Carolina Press in 1970.

II

SOME familiarity with traditional ideas about metaphor and its relation to imagination, knowledge, and other subjects is essential to understanding the novelty and significance of the idea of metaphor expressed by Shelley in the *Defence*. His view of it is directly and radically opposed to the common opinion that metaphor is a beguiling species of equivocation, delightful and useful rhetorically for purposes of persuasion and illustration but in the last analysis an enemy to instruction and sound judgment. Generally speaking, within this neo-classical tradition, the real foundation of all (secular) instruction, mimetic and discursive alike, is that complex of Reason and Nature which can be called the world system. The basic unit of instruction in the universe of discourse which has the world system as its object is the univocal statement or proposition which can be cashed in, like a bank note, for phenomena. Such a transaction constitutes a claim to knowledge. These and related beliefs and procedures, which will be considered further when it is important to establish a context for positions expressed in the *Defence*, represent some of the laws and reigning opinions of the tyrannous universe of discourse which Shelley, like Blake, and, more cautiously, Coleridge, sought to depose in favor of a universe of poetry: an imaginative cosmos at once more adequately centered in immediate experience and more open to creative myth at the circumference of human knowledge.

Coleridge himself accurately reflects received opinion about metaphor. At the start of a famous passage in *The Statesman's Manual* which defines the concept of a symbol and which looks, as Shelley was to do, beyond the division of science and poetry, he observes:

> *Eheu! paupertina in paupertinam religionem ducit:* -- A hunger-bitten and idea-less philosophy naturally produces a starveling and comfortless religion. It is among the miseries of the present age that it recognizes no *medium* between literal and metaphorical. Faith is either to be buried in the dead letter, or its name and honors usurped by a counterfeit product of the mechanical understanding, which in the blindness of self-complacency confounds symbols with allegories. [1]

Common seventeenth- and eighteenth-century attitudes toward language and its relation to reason and imagination fostered the dilemma of scriptural interpretation Coleridge thus laments, and they are variously evident in the following passages by Thomas Sprat, John Locke, and Isaac Watts, respectively:

> They make the *Fancy* disgust the best things, if they come sound and unadorn'd: they are in open defiance against *Reason;* professing, not to hold much correspondence with that; but with its Slaves *the Passions:* they give the mind a motion too changeable, and bewitching, to consist with *right practice.* Who can behold, without indignation, how many mists and uncertainties, these specious *Tropes* and *Figures* have brought on our knowledge? How many rewards, which are due to more profitable and difficult *arts,* have been still snatch'd away by the easy vanity of *fine speaking?* For now I am warmed with this anger, I cannot with-hold my self, from betraying the shallowness of all these seeming Mysteries; upon which, we *Writers,* and *Speakers,* look so bigg, And, in few words, I dare say; that of all the Studies of men, nothing may be sooner obtained, than this vicious abundance of *Phrase,* this trick of *Metaphors,* this volubility of Tongue, which makes so great a noise in the World. [2]

[1] *The Statesman's Manual* (London, 1816), p. 36.
[2] As quoted from *The History of the Royal Society of London* (London, 1667), p. 112 by W.S. Howell in *Logic and Rhetoric in England, 1500-1700* (New York, 1961), p. 389.

.   .   .   .

For wit lying most in the assemblage of ideas, and put-
ting those together with quickness and variety wherein
can be found any resemblance or congruity, thereby to
make up pleasant pictures and agreeable visions in the
fancy: Judgement, on the contrary, lies quite on the
other side, in separating carefully one from another
ideas wherein can be found the least difference, thereby
to avoid being mislead by similitude, and by affinity to
take one thing for another. This is a way of proceeding
quite contrary to metaphor and allusion, wherein for
the most part lies that entertainment and pleasantry of
wit which strikes so lively on the fancy, and therefore is
so acceptable to all the people; because its beauty appears at first sight, and there is required no labor of
thought to examine what truth or reason there is in it.
The mind, without looking any farther, rests satisfied
with the agreeableness of the picture and the gaiety of
the fancy: and it is a kind of an affront to go about to
examine it by the severe rules of truth and good reason;
whereby it appears that it consists in something that is
not perfectly conformable to them. [3]

.   .   .   .

Equivocal words are in the forth place distinguish'd
by their *literal* or *Figurative* Sense. Words are used in a
proper or *literal* Sense, when they are design'd to signify
those Ideas for which they were originally made, or to
which they are primarily generally annexed; but they
are used in a *figurative* or *tropical* Sense, when they are
made to signify some things, which only bear either a
Reference or a Resemblance to the Primary Ideas of
them.

Here *note,* That the Design of *metaphorical Language* and *Figures of Speech* is not merely to represent
our Ideas, but to represent them with *Vivacity, Spirit,*

[3] *An Essay Concerning Human Understanding* (Oxford,
1924), p. 86.

Affection, and *Power;* and tho they make a deeper Impression on the Mind of the Hearer, yet they do as often lead him into a Mistake, if they are used at improper Times and Places. Therefore, where the design of the Speaker or Writer is merely to *explain,* to *instruct,* and to lead into the knowledge of the naked Truth, he ought, for the most part to use *plain* and *proper* Words, if the Language affords them, and not to deal much in *figurative Speech.* But this sort of terms is used very profitably by Poets and Orators, whose business is to move, and persuade and work on the Passions, as well as on the Understanding.[4]

Sprat's reproach is directed to false wits among scientific writers, but his attitude toward metaphor is rooted in ancient psychological and metaphysical distinctions between reason and fancy, judgment and wit, being and seeming which appear clearly in Locke's account. There truth is the province of discursive or intuitive reason and inferential discourse; enjoyment or pleasure is the province of the passions, fancy, and the associations of ideas (and ideas virtually personified as they were to be later in the surrealistic hedonism of the utilitarians). By the time David Hume had set it down that "reason is and ought to be the slave of the passions,"[5] the concepts of mind, the world system, and language evident in Watts's statement were in principle bankrupt but it was many years, even to the twentieth century, before a sure challenge was delivered to the last of these.[6]

Shelley's interpretation of Hume, Berkeley, Sir Wil-

[4] *Logick: or the Right Use of Reason in the Enquiry after Truth* (London, 1736), pp. 64-65.

[5] *A Treatise of Human Nature,* ed. L.A. Selby-Bigge (Oxford, 1967), p. 415.

[6] Cf. I.A. Richards, *The Philosophy of Rhetoric* (New York, 1936), and Willard Van Orman Quine, *From a Logical Point of View* (Cambridge, 1953), especially "Two Dogmas of Empiricism," pp. 20-46 and "The Problem of Meaning in Linguistics," pp. 47-64.

liam Drummond, and others, including Coleridge, ena-
bled him, as we shall see later on, to participate very
clear-headedly in the implications of the empiricist rev-
olution in philosophy and to conceive a profoundly different attitude toward metaphor, one which did not, in
fact, find a viable place in Anglo-American thought until recent decades.[7] From his time to ours aversion or
adulation for a poet's opposition to soulless rationalism
commonly spelled inattention to his sophisticated conception of the philosophic and critical traditions of British thought in which his mind developed. Yet the
Defence is charged both with these native problems and
premises and with perceptively ironic uses of current
imagery and terminology; he recognized the poverty of
imagination in prevailing conceptions of reason, senti-
ment, sensation, pleasure, utility, calculation, nature,
and poetry. His reactions to these standardized usages
comprise leitmotifs which run throughout the argument
and vision of his main theme of transvaluation of the
coherent yet hollow system delivered by the enlighten-
ment rationalists. Metaphor, as the passages above may
suggest, is one of the concepts through which he found
an alternative vision; imagination, as we shall see, is another.

Shelley's statement that "Reason is the enumeration
of quantities already known" (*D,* VII, 109) must also be
understood against the background of seventeenth- and
eighteenth-century empiricism. It is a minimal and
grudging and, at first sight, an obscure description of
the activity Coleridge had come to regard as the province of the fancy and the understanding. It can be para-
phrased in the form of a corollary: "rationality is the
logico-mathematical manipulation of determinate, nor-

[7] Cf. Richards, Turbayne, and also Mary B. Hesse, "The Ex-
planatory Function of Metaphor," in *International Congress for
Logic, Methodology, and Philosophy of Science,* ed. Y. Bar-
Hillel (Amsterdam, 1955), p. 253 ff.

malized phenomena in univocal language." When he adds that "imagination is the perception of the value of those quantities, both separately and as a whole" (*D,* VII, 109), Shelley is not saying that the determinate phenomena and units of their expression can be placed on a scale of worth, relative, say, to the end of human happiness as the utilitarians of his time were claiming; he is asserting that aesthesis is primitive and that it is first and finally only about values that man thinks. And he continues his innovation by citing a traditional principle whose values he is actually reversing, "Reason respects the differences, imagination the similitudes of things" (*D,* VII, 109). By claiming epistemological priority for imagination Shelley turns one of the central principles of the Baconian-Lockean theory of knowledge against the theory of mind it started from: reason or judgment becomes the instrument only, not the agent of knowledge; imagination (or what some earlier authors called wit) produces all the material and constitutes the bloom of human knowledge. His new view of metaphor reveals clearly the nature of the imaginative process and, as he sees it, the true condition of human knowledge. [8]

[8] It has more and more become the tendency of modern thought to regard all things and principles of things as metaphors operating in the cosmos of human culture in various states of animation and decay. The extent and awareness of this tendency is indicated by Nelson Goodman's witty recent question, "Is a metaphor, then, simply a juvenile fact and a fact simply a senile metaphor?" (*The Languages of Art,* New York, 1968, p. 68). He adds, "That needs some modification but does argue against excluding the metaphorical from the actual. Metaphorical possession is indeed not *literal* possession; but possession is actual whether metaphorical or literal." Owen Barfield has noted the growth of interest "in the last few decades [in] this whole question of the figurative make-up of collective representations" (*Saving the Appearances,* New York, 1957, p. 28). He clearly regards the languages of art or culture as poetry in Shelley's sense: "Participation is the extrasensory relation between man and the phenomena" (p.40). The actual is always a collective representation, a composition.

The *Defence* contains only one extended direct account of metaphor, but that single statement has an integral position. It was demonstrably designed to express key elements of the theory of mind and experience upon which Shelley built his constructive argument—and to reflect the impoverished traditional views of language, imagination, and poetry he attacked. When the essential connections are seen between the following passage and his other better known statements about thought, imagination, poetry, and society (and they have not so far been noted in the literature on Shelley), it becomes amply clear that all metaphor, in perception, thought, and language alike, depends for its existence and effect on creative acts of relational apprehension.

> Their language is vitally metaphorical, that is it marks the before unapprehended relations of things and perpetuates their apprehension until the words which represent them become, through time, signs for portions and classes of thought instead of [what they are originally] pictures of integral thoughts; and then if no new poets should arise to create afresh the associations which have been thus dis*organ*ized, language will be dead to all the nobler purposes of human intercourse. (*D,* VII, 111; italics mine)

All claims to knowledge in the universe of discourse which Shelley attacks involve a basic forgetfulness (1) of the synthetic character of the apprehended relations of things from which they arise, and (2) of the metaphoric character of the languages in which they find continuing expression. With Berkeley and Hume—and for Shelley—the metaphysical fiction of correspondence between mind and Nature is overthrown by the genius of experience itself. Reason's kingship ends and the inheritors of all that is best, most loving, and generous in human purposes resides with the poets "in the most universal sense of the word." In terms of Shelley's philosophic position the chief, and as far as I can tell, the most novel, idea in the *Defence* is the view expressed here that metaphor is a direct agent of human knowledge which picks out and perpetuates the apprehension of things or relations of things otherwise invisible to or overlooked by the human mind at any point in its individual or cultural history. In this sense metaphor is both the record and the vehicle of human discovery. (In our own time some philosophers of science are urging that metaphors or models are necessary and not merely heuristic elements of theoretical discovery and explanation of certain kinds.[9]) Without its central concept of metaphoric apprehension of relations between "impressions" or the elements of experience, the *Defence* would have lacked what was most essential to its argument: an account of how or in what sense imagination produces knowledge.

First, negatively, the idea that a metaphor is a picture of an integral thought is immediately significant by contrast with the notion that a dead metaphor is a mere sign for homogenized portions and classes of thought no longer understood or, what amounts to the same thing, no longer apprehended as something synthesized or unified by the mind. In this decadent condition metaphor is tyrannous; it is received and used only as a univocal name or other part of speech for things and relations of things not in themselves integral or homogenous. "The victim of metaphor," as C.M. Turbayne observes, "accepts one way of sorting or bundling or allocating the facts as the only way to sort, bundle or allocate them . . . he confuses a special view of the world with the world."[10] Positively, the idea that metaphor is an integral form of apprehension and expression enunciates the principle that the mind, initially and finally, decides how relations of things are to be regarded, usu-

[9] Cf. Hesse, p. 253 ff.
[10] Cf. Turbayne, p. 27.

ally by the simple expedient of so regarding them. Metaphor is organized language and thought in the sense that the reason for or unifying principle of the relations it discovers is immediately evident in the unified verbal formula or other form of expression. The phrases "metal fatigue," "genetic code," "time's scythe," and (as applied to Mussolini by Churchill) "that utensil" are examples of such integral expression of previously unapprehended relations of things. [11] Another good example of such a formula is the now largely dead metaphor "wind stream" which will be examined when Shelley's own use of metaphor is considered. Before we turn to his practice and to other aspects of his account of metaphor, however, it is important to establish more precisely the sense in which he uses the concept of integral thought, for it is the defining characteristic of metaphor in apprehension and expression alike.

The language of poets in the general sense is *vitally metaphoric* in that it marks organized, integral relations of things apprehended by the mind. To the extent that a poet, like a computer, only manipulates "fixities and definites," the referents of the univocation theory of language, his work will amount only to a species of the false wit described by Joseph Addison or to the merely fanciful permutations of codified notions attacked in somewhat different terms but with similar intent by Wordsworth and Coleridge a century later. Coleridge particularly had demonstrated to Shelley and a few other readers that the poetry of the fancy and the religion, philosophy, science, and ethics of the understanding had become void of significance and of that integral unity craved by the mind and heart of man. His distinctions between imagination and the fancy and between reason and the understanding correspond very closely to the distinction between reason and the imagination

[11] Cf. Turbayne, pp. 12-14 ff.

which opens Shelley's *Defence.* By reason Shelley meant what Coleridge, following the Germans, had called the understanding and, as its aesthetic counterpart, the fancy; by imagination Shelley meant what Coleridge distinguished as reason in its coadunative aesthetic manifestation, imagination. Shelley's definitions describe the productive and organizing power of imagination (not its status as a Kantian faculty) in terms of the same principle of integration on which he bases his conception of vitally metaphoric language. Taken together, these ideas of metaphor and imagination define a capacity for metaphoric apprehension which he considered to be the fundamental power of the human mind and a mental counterpart of the primal capacity for self-transcendence he found in love.

> According to one mode of regarding those two classes of mental action called reason and imagination, the former may be considered as mind contemplating the relations borne by one thought to another, however produced; and the latter as mind acting on those thoughts so as to color them with its own light, *and composing from them, as from elements, other thoughts, each containing within itself the principle of its own integrity.* (*D,* VII, 109; italics mine)

By a thought Shelley means here, as elsewhere, anything attended to by the mind. He accepted the epistemological position, as we shall see, that man has no knowledge whatever beyond what the mind attends to. His own chief conclusion from this position is two-sided: (1) that "the relations of things remain unchanged whatever the [philosophic] system" (*OL,* VI, 196) and (2) that the composition of thoughts from other thoughts is a creative unifying process immediately expressive of the mind's own nature and effected necessarily with awareness of the reason and nature of the thoughts thus unified. The first of these conclusions determines the function of reason and the scope of discursive, scientific knowledge indicated in the preceding passage. The second conclusion indicates the character of the aesthetic epistemology Shelley developed from the conviction that skeptical empiricism had shown the impossibility of knowing the reason and nature of any objective phenomena. The opening paragraphs of the *Defence* show his recognition that the philosophic alternatives lay in agnostic scientific operationalism and in a psychological and cultural phenomenalism which respects mind as a maker and for what it makes. Throughout the *Defence* he acknowledges the ancient dualism of these human powers and purposes, and attempts to identify their proper and compatible functions as part of his answer to rationalistic reductionism.

Shelley goes on to say at the start that reason, "the principle of analysis . . . regards the relations of things simply as relations; considering thoughts, not in their integral [and mind-made] unity but as algebraical relations which conduct to certain general results" (*D*, VII, 109). On the surface, this may appear as one of the more obscure statements in the *Defence*. But considered in the context of Shelley's good understanding of eighteenth-century British philosophy, and of Sir William Drummond's *Academical Questions*, it provides one good source of current reflections on the question of what skeptical empiricism made of the scope of scientific inquiry. [12] Therefore it becomes clear that Shelley has in mind man's scientific calculations of the regular processes of nature and projects of society. These conduce to "certain general results" through the collection of data about the relations between phenomena. By experimental manipulation of such data, constant and variable elements of phenomena are made apparent and

[12] Sir William Drummond, *Academical Questions* (London, 1805), pp. 3 and 195-206.

a kind of grammar of nature and policy develops. Beyond such operational knowledge, urged by Newton for "experimental philosophy" [13] and worked out as a scientific methodology with great sophistication by Bishop Berkeley, lie the meta-scientific questions of what had been called "natural philosophy"—ontological questions about the elements of general theory insofar as it goes beyond the results and procedures of experiment and observation. [14] Clearly, regarding "relations as relations" involves no consideration of the ontological status, the truth or falsity, or the integrity or heterogeneity of the things investigated. In Shelley's view imagination alone is productive of the higher reaches of scientific as well as poetic myth—and not of the higher reaches only but of every significant, integral transformation in the forms of human apprehension.

Shelley's statements about the integrative power of imagination clarify his definition of metaphor and indicate that metaphor is a vital form of language only to the extent that it is first a specific form of relational apprehension. Metaphors consist of relations synthesized by imagination from the elements of experience. Experience consists of these syntheses. Nelson Goodman, in whose philosophic thought empiricism and platonism are also singularly united, has put it this way: "the 'natural' kinds are simply those we are in the habit of picking out for and by labeling. Moreover, the object itself is not ready-made but results from a way of taking the world." [15] Whether the elements of experience are regarded as philosophic universals or as the particulars of sensation, perception, or thought, they are united by and for the mind and in their integrity are as organisms of mental life. The character of these creatures of the life of the mind can be learned concretely from Shelley's

---

13 *Opticks* (New York, 1952), pp. 404-405.

14 Ibid., pp. 404-405 and Turbayne, pp. 40-45 and 208-217.

15 Goodman, p. 32.

poetry as we shall see later; it can also be indicated by
adapting and expanding a traditional organic metaphor
of breeding or crossbreeding.

In apprehending and expressing "before unapprehended [or forgotten] relations of things," imagination
crosses the so-called natural

l kinds, the given elements of thought and language
which make up a world for the mind, and thus produces
hybrid thoughts and expressions of thought which, either in themselves or as they are generalized, disrupt
and enliven the system of mental and linguistic habits
into which they are assimilated.[16] Some of these hybrids
are more viable than others, since they have greater
scope or integrity for the mind. For philosophic reasons
(which will be considered later here after other aspects
of his concept of metaphor have been examined) Shelley regarded this process of mental ontogenesis as the
process of world-making. His position animates and
generalizes the notion of *poesis* to the point of regarding
the world as a mind-made poem in which metaphor is
tantamount to metamorphosis and imagination is the
agent of transfiguration in human nature. Perceiving
one thing as or as if it were another—like speaking of
one thing in idioms appropriate to another thing—
involves a form of mental activity in which the mind
can become immediately aware of the nature of its own
synthetic activity. Once Shelley's idea of the integrative
function of imagination is clear, in its existential as well
as its epistemological implications, his idea of the noetic
efficacy and organizing function of metaphor can be
understood as the essential vehicle of the symbolic
transformations by which reality for the mind is constructed.

In certain respects Shelley's account of metaphor

[16] Shelley's conception and use of myth is studied in the two
following sections.

and his uses of the terms metaphor and symbol in his later poetry show striking similarity to the remarkable definition of a symbol Coleridge put in *The Statesman's Manual* (1816). Shelley apparently had read the definition:

> Now an allegory is but a translation of abstract notions into a picture-language, which is itself nothing but an abstraction from objects of the senses; the principal being more worthless even than its phantom proxy, both alike unsubstantial, and the former shapeless to boot. On the other hand a symbol . . . is characterized by a translucence of the special in the individual, or of the general in the special, or of the universal in the general; above all by the translucence of the eternal through and in the temporal. It always partakes of the reality which it renders intelligible; and while it enunciates the whole, abides itself as a living part in that unity of which it is the representative. [17]

Since metaphor and symbol do not figure significantly as concepts in Shelley's prose or poetry before 1818, it may well be that this passage gave him the idea of symbolic and vital—as against rhetorical and dead—metaphor he needed for his own theory of imagination as the prime agent of *poesis.* The idea of figurative apprehension and expression of reality for the mind is present in Coleridge's definition, and it would be surprising if it were to be found at all in then-current theories of language or in traditional rhetoric. And Shelley's own phrase, "pictures of integral thoughts," has the appearance of a synthesis of the elements of Coleridge's statement. However the question of indebtedness may stand, the two positions are significant analogues of a comparatively novel idea. For an epistemology of aesthetics the heart of Coleridge's statement is the notion

[17] Coleridge, p. 36-37. On Shelley's reading see *The Letters of Percy Bysshe Shelley,* ed. F.L. Jones (Oxford, 1964), II, 472.

that the symbol—not the verbal or other physical sign, but the idea signified by it—participates in the higher, less evident, less familiar reality which it illuminates and renders intelligible. A symbol lets light into discourse. An allegory (in Coleridge's sense) only reflects available light, as with a set of mirrors.

Shelley's definition of metaphor expresses the idea that the relations marked in vital metaphor are integrally coherent and participate in a new reality for the mind, one not given to it by sensation or reason, nature, or culture. For him, as for Coleridge, the figure, metaphor or symbol, initiates transcendence and directly informs the mind about what is real for it. How such metaphoric apprehension transfigures individual experience or a cultural tradition constitutes one of the central features of Shelley's myth of metaphor, and it will be examined in the next section and illustrated in the conclusion of this study. His later poetry offers many valuable illustrations of his leading idea of the integrity of relationships unified by metaphor as apprehended by the mind.

A passage from *Epipsychidion* (1821), one apparently neoplatonic in perspective and closely related to the mythography of *Adonais* and *Prometheus Unbound*, provides a kind of ostensive definition for us of Shelley's idea of metaphor:

> See where she stands! a mortal shape indeed
> With love and life and deity,
> And motion which can change but cannot die;
> An image of some bright Eternity;
> A shadow of some golden dream; a Splendour
> Leaving the third sphere pilotless; a tender
> Reflection of the eternal Moon of Love
> Under whose motions life's dull billows move;
> A Metaphor of Spring and Youth and Morning;
> A vision like incarnate April, warning,
> With smiles and tears, Frost the Anatomy
> Into his summer grave. (II, 110)

The succession of these images carefully and conventionally descends from the One to the grave of not-being but not, as later discussion will more fully show, with the purpose of invoking the neoplatonic scale of being and locating the angelic beloved in the plastic sweep of a transcendent world. The perspective is subjective, idealist, phenomenological—the images are treated as relations which elicit the speaker's apprehension of an ineffable presence in the woman. Her presence, commingled with the poet's mind, participates in all things of value. The line "A Metaphor of Spring and Youth and Morning" indicates that she is herself a metaphor expressively embodying for the poet's mind the relations of spring to the year, youth to life, and morning to the day. English has no word for the integral or unifying element of these relations, though it might well have. And if there were such a term or phrase it would, Shelley says, in time cease to be a picture of the integral set of relations he expresses in this passage and become a name or sign for a "thing," a so-called objective quality, property or substance. Thus Shelley's line marks in vital metaphor "before unapprehended relations of things and perpetuates their apprehension," just as Emilia Viviani, a metaphor in the universe of poetry, creates an eternity in time for the communion of imagination by the vital expression of ineffable relations which transcend the systems of nature and culture.

Another vivid illustration of Shelley's concept of metaphor, one which even more fully and immediately suggests the sophistication of his insight, is the famous image of the "tangled boughs of Heaven and Ocean" in *Ode to the West Wind*. It is impossible to suppose that Shelley synthesized the images of the following passage and regarded them as the vehicle for his own sense of awe and terror over mutability, without a clear sense of mixing or joining the relations of quite distinct yet analogous phenomena:

Thou on whose stream, mid the steep sky's commotion,
Loose clouds like earth's decaying leaves are shed,
Shook from the tangled boughs of Heaven and Ocean

Angels of rain and lightning: there are spread. . . . (II,
295)

It was noted earlier that "wind-stream" is now a dead
metaphor in English. Though Shelley's image is famous
and generally well understood, it may be useful to observe that the base of his metaphor is the phenomenon
of the westerly autumn wind shaking leaves from tangled boughs onto a stream. The first tenor is the imaginative figure of the seasonal commotion of the sky's
shaking of clouds from the tangled systems of water and
air onto the stream of the wind in accordance with the
principles of evaporation and condensation. The second
tenor, if we accept that Shelley here, as elsewhere, aims
to break down the useful habit of distinguishing between the perceiver and the perceived, involves the
mind's commotion as some awful change, perhaps of
mood, is felt. It is that vivid and (without metaphor) in-
describable apprehension which the other better-known
relations serve. The west wind and the commotion of
the sky and the mind are analogous principles which
hold the relations together in an integral unity.

Another very important aspect of Shelley's account
of metaphor is his description of what we can call the
semantic entropy principle. When "before unapprehended relations of things" are marked by a metaphor,
and while the metaphor is fresh and our perception of
its relations is a vivid, feeling one, the mind is, so to
speak, in close touch with the basic conditions of learning and knowing. In Shelley's account such imaginative
relational or analogical apprehension is as basic to
learning as direct sensation; and it is surely as basic as
the sense of mental sight and security of order which accompanies, and has sometimes been made the criterion

for, deductive inference.[18] In poetry, in his general sense, the aesthesis in immediate perception of the elements of thought is an effect of bringing thoughts, again in his general sense, into a relationship which is novel relative to our fixed knowledge, indeterminate relative to our standard usage, and yet somehow better known than our beliefs and more determinate than our instrumental and univocally categorical uses of language. The metaphor is an organized apprehension, and it organizes or reorganizes consciousness as long as its relations are apprehended. The belief that it disorganizes knowledge holds only when the relations are forgotten or not noticed. But, as Shelley points out, a metaphor becomes in time a "sign for portions or classes of thought" and awareness of the relationships it has marked declines into an opaque familiarity with its general use. The sign, which once signified, becomes in time the thing signified—as when a person is called a red, a black, or a white. "Before unapprehended relations," once nothing for the mind, emerge in metaphor as novel, immediate, and integral apprehensions and then slide into dotage as entities in a world system.

Thus, singly taken, metaphorical words become dead metaphors and, more generally, the great myths and metaphors of religion, philosophy, science, art, politics, and so on become literal and often preposterous repre-

18 Descartes and Locke both described intuition as a principle of intellectual decorum, a fundamental power of mind to recognize thoughts which necessarily fit or go together. Shelley has this primitive mental initiative in mind when he describes man as "an instrument over which a series of external and internal impressions are driven like the alternations of an ever changing wind over an Aeolian lyre which move it by their motion to everchanging melody. But there is a principle within the human being, and perhaps within all sentient beings, which acts otherwise than in a lyre and produces not the sounds and motions thus excited to the impressions which excite them" (*D*, VII, 109). This adjustment must occur through the two modes of "mental action," reason and imagination (*D*, VII, 109).

sentation. [19] The catalogue of dead metaphor is virtually inexhaustible. Semantic entropy is the principle that the elements of cognitive and emotive organization tend through time, like all other forms of energy, toward disorganization of the relationships once unified or integrally apprehended: imagined and felt, to use Shelley's terms. Metaphors become "signs for portions and classes of thought instead of pictures of integral thoughts; and then if no new poets should arise to create afresh the associations [that is to re-imagine the integral relationships] which have thus been disorganized, language [and theories, works of art, and institutions] will be dead to all the nobler purposes of human intercourse" (*D,* VII, 111). That is, language and (to include what is clearly implied by Shelley's position) the other symbolic forms of human culture, will be dead to feeling and imagining and through these to knowing, loving, and the communion of communication. Discourse is intercourse when it has imagination, as opinion is knowledge when one knows the reason for the fact.

From what has been established up to this point it should be clear that metaphor is the basic event or element of imaginative apprehension—and that because imagination is the primitive and primary activity of the human mind, metaphor must be the basic unit and genetic principle of the world poem which constitutes reality for the mind. Without awareness of the centrality of metaphor in experience, human nature is imprisoned in its own synthetic activity, taking as literal and external things ("thoughts") made up out of its own inner nature. Shelley's myth of metaphor rivals the myth that the mind is only a passive recipient of external messages transmitted to it in a code which can be broken only by

[19] One of the more accessible fascinations of Norman O. Brown's *Love's Body* (New York, 1968) is his genius for resurrecting the moribund elements of the great metaphors and myths which direct western civilization.

eliminating as so much noise the proper and necessarily metaphoric apprehensions of the mind. His position implies a far-reaching analogy between the nature of the artist and his composition: each reflects and expresses the other, and together they constitute the only world real for the mind. [20]

Whereas the divine artificer of the Newtonians and Deists had become a mechanic, the artificer of the world poem is a poet who exists for man only when his own imaginative activity is recognized through awareness of metaphor to constitute the world of his immediate experience. One of the many passages which express this position in the *Defence* naturally requires the reader to go back to its opening definitions and to the passages on metaphor and the process of artistic generation:

> Language, color, form, and religious and civil habits of action, are all instruments and materials of poetry; they may be called poetry by that figure of speech which considers the effect as a synonym of the cause. (*D,* VII, 113)

Language, color, form, and religious and civil habits of action are the effects of poetry—that is, of the synthetic activity of imagination. They are the instruments and materials of poetry in the sense of Shelley's original definition: imagination is "mind acting upon those thoughts [the materials and instruments of poetry] so as to color them with its own light and composing from them as from elements, other thoughts [metaphors, poems, paintings, sculptures, music, myths and laws and institutions] each containing within itself [originally] the principles of its own integrity" (*D,* VII, 109). We need only add one assumption, which later will be

[20] This point is considered more fully in relation to *Adonais* in the conclusion of this essay.

demonstrated, to be sure of this interpretation of the two passages: that the "instruments and materials of poetry" are "thoughts" for the mind in Shelley's (largely Berkeleyan) sense. From "before unapprehended relations of things" imagination synthesizes the "thoughts" which are the materials and instruments of poetry, and these in turn become the fabric of poetry in the public sense in all its forms in human culture. The process is one of continuous reciprocal transformation and does not admit of reduction of the syntheses which make up poetry or culture to any set of sterilized atomic sensations or univocal linguistic entities. The mind cannot, except by ignoring its primary activity, get beyond the metaphoric syntheses which constitute the "thoughts" (things) of its immediate experience.

The crucial points follow from my earlier discussion. The language of poets is vitally metaphorical, and the materials and instruments of poetry are themselves a vitally metaphorical language in Shelley's sense of "before unapprehended relations of things" apprehended synthetically by imagination and containing in themselves, as apprehended, the principles of their own integrity. What is known or familiar to a culture and an individual constantly inclines, in accordance with the semantic entropy principle, to the condition of dead metaphor. If the foregoing argument has correctly generalized the logic of Shelley's definitions of metaphor and imagination, it follows that culture is intrinsically and entirely poetry for the mind and that reality as distinct from human culture is simply a notion which results from taking metaphor literally or allowing the mind's metaphors to become disorganized. His distinctive sense of the drama of cultural poesis is beautifully exemplified in an account of the power of imagination to make living myth from the radically metaphoric materials of history.

The true poetry of Rome lived in its institutions; for whatever of beautiful, true, and majestic, they contained, could have sprung only from the faculty which creates the order in which they consisted. . . .

At length the ancient system of religion and manners had fulfilled the circle of its revolutions. And the world would have fallen into utter anarchy and darkness, but that there were found poets among the authors of the Christian and chivalric systems of manners and religion, who created forms of opinion and action never before conceived; which, copied into the imaginations of men, became as generals to the bewildered armies of their thoughts. (*D,* VII, 125)

Shelley's position in the *Defence* substitutes a world poem for the world system and a universe of poetry for the universe of discourse in accordance with the epistemological principle that "all things exist as they are perceived, at least in relation to the percipient" (*D,* VII, 137); and this substitution is made on the assumption that it is morally and spiritually better for the individual actively to feel what he perceives and to imagine what he knows than for him to acquiesce passively to an order which he neither perceives nor knows. In these terms and broadly speaking, what science and the conventions of standard social and linguistic usage provide does not resemble closely, if it resembles at all, the realities of individual experience. The forgotten relations of things which were once the reasons or integrating principles of systems of opinion and forms of conduct are recoverable only by an imaginative act, never by a ratiocinative one—as computer technology is now demonstrating. Immediate experience itself, in Shelley's view, is radically metaphoric; and the art of knowing and the art of poetry are one in the sense that man makes the things he wants to know about and the means of finding out about them. Of course, naively and "literally" interpreted, this creative or aesthetic epistemology may seem inclined toward anarchy and solipsistic regression; but Shelley does not imply that the individual should create a personal world in this way. (*Alastor* shows the fascination and futility of taking metaphors literally.) He argues rather from the position that man exists unavoidably in such a personal world and that he should recognize, if he can, first, the helpless passivity of his relationship to any—perforce imaginatively generated—world system unimaginatively received and, secondly, that all his learning and all that he calls desirable depend directly on the activity of his own imagination defined as the activity of making from the radically metaphorical fabric of his experience the forms of perceiving and knowing he calls his world.

III

THE IDEA that poetry, the *poema* of any *poesis,* [21] is reality for the mind, that it originates in what has been called here metaphoric relational apprehension, and that it manifests itself in human culture in vitally metaphoric language, takes on the lineaments of myth where Shelley treats imagination as the soul of the cultural process and as the means of self-transcendence, of grace in the universe of poetry. [22] The primary vehicle of his expression of this myth is the image of consciousness as a circle or radiating field. To understand the scope of this image or model and to see the myth clearly it is necessary to understand the philosophic underpinnings and the dynamics of his notion of imaginative transformation. The imagery with which he synthesized his views on imagination, poetry, and metaphor in the *Defence* leads directly into both of these areas. For example, when he explains how "imagination is the great instrument of moral good," he first introduces the figure of the circle to organize his expression of the transformational and regenerative processes of imagination:

[21] Schulze uses this distinction for his analysis of the poetics of the *Defence.*

[22] In this and the following chapter uses of the term myth accord with suggestions made by Henry A. Murray in "The Possible Nature of a 'Mythology' to Come," in *Myth and Mythmaking,* ed. Murray (Boston, 1968), pp. 349-350. He writes: "A myth never reproduces the perception of a specific, overt (historical) event, and hence it is never true or false in these terms. Its function is to evoke a total empathic experience of the essential features of a series of prototypical events, often accompanied by the belief that conduct should be guided (activated or inhibited) by this vicarious experience. Here 'truth' may mean, 'essentially and importantly true to life,' or 'true value,' 'true path,' or 'true goal.'"

> Poetry enlarges the circumference of the imagination by
> replenishing it with thoughts of ever new delight, which
> have the power of attracting and assimilating to their
> own nature all other thoughts and which form new in-
> tervals and interstices whose void forever craves fresh
> food. (*D,* VII, 118)

Here, to use a phrase of Shelley's, "by that figure of
speech which considers the effect as a synonym of the
cause" (*D,* VII, 113), imagination means the whole field
of reality apprehended metaphorically and "in relation
to the percipient." We have seen earlier that he regards
poetry's "thoughts of ever new delight" primarily as integral metaphoric relations continually unfolding in accordance with certain mental principles which he calls
"the permanent analogy of things" (*D,* VII, 116).

The circle image and the coordinate images of a web
(or network) and a process of transformations radiating
from a center were dominant organizing devices of his
thought in the great creative period between 1818 and
1821. Imagery of a "magic circle" gradually displaces
imagery of the cave. It is present in his prose pieces as a
metaphor for mind and it has a very important role in
the *Witch of Atlas, Epipsychidion,* and *Hellas* and in
the mental imagery which integrates the cosmic drama
of *Prometheus Unbound.* In *Adonais,* as we shall see,
the circle image and the metaphor of passage from center to the circumference correspond as they should,
given Shelley's philosophic position, to the elegist's
point of view; and they appear at the climactic point of
his own conversion to direct experience or acceptance
of the myth of transfiguration he has created in the
elegy. And, throughout his poem, imagery of flower,
song, and star comprise a network of metaphoric relations harmonized and unified in an original way in accordance with the "permanent analogy" available to
Shelley in the concept of radiation. These images are in-

deed conventional features of the elegy; but Shelley, following closely his own idea of metaphor, has revived or discovered the permanent analogy in their relations of radial unfolding or expansion; and he uses the images as a kind of family of integrating metaphors in the poem's scheme of transfiguration.[23]

In the *Defence,* however, Shelley's concern is less with the rites of passage between center and circumference than with the nature, the origin, end, and structure, of imaginative experience and with the principles of the cosmic scheme used in his greater poetry. He uses the circle and related images to express both the relations of conversion between old and new thoughts and the principle of transformation and transfiguration provided by his concept of metaphor. The heterogeneous and suggestive imagery of his argument requires, and fortunately his earlier prose provides, an account of the concept of mind and the theory of experience from which his aesthetic epistemology derives. When his acute and often brilliant reflections on the principles and implications of eighteenth-century British philosophy are understood, the coherence, power, and originality of his position are much more evident.

In the essay *On Life* and in the fragmentary essay *Speculations on Metaphysics,* the epistemological principles of the Intellectual Philosophy upon which the *Defence* is based are very clearly expressed. The distinction already considered, for example, between the modes of reason and imagination is, given Shelley's later idea of the synthetic and integrative power of imagination, a transformation of the distinction between metaphysics and logic in the first of the following paragraphs.

---

[23] Cf. Earl R. Wasserman's fine analysis of the imagery of *Adonais* in *The Subtler Language.* As indicated in Chapter IV, however, he does not relate Shelley's practice to the *Defence.*

Metaphysics may be defined as the science of all that we know, feel, remember, and believe inasmuch as our knowledge, sensations, memory and faith constitute the universe relatively to human identity. Logic or the science of words, must no longer be confounded with the science of facts. Words are the instruments of mind whose capacities it becomes the metaphysician accurately to know, but they are not mind, nor are they portions of mind. (*SM,* VII, 63)

Most of the errors of philosophers have arisen from considering the human being from a point of view too detailed and circumscribed [a camera]. He is not [only] a moral and an intellectual—but also and pre-eminently an imaginative being. His own mind is all things to him. If we would arrive at any knowledge which would be serviceable from the practical conclusions to which it leads, we ought to consider the mind of man and the universe as the great whole on which to exercise our speculations. . . . It imports little to inquire whether thought be distinct from the objects thought. (*SM,* VII, 65)

In the second of these paragraphs, as in the *Defence,* imagination is regarded as the activity in which the human mind begins and ends. Its suggestion of continuity between thought and the objects of thought already anticipates the theory of experience as imaginative transformation of metaphor. Starting, as Berkeley, Hume, and others had urged, with careful study of the content of immediate experience, Shelley regards the mind as a dynamic field containing "thoughts" in various relations and states of clarity. Throughout this field, from the most evanescent and particular to the most stable and universal of these thoughts, imagination is the operative power when man is not confining his activity to manipulations of the language and grammar of science. Imagination creates, and makes it possible to discover in previous creations, the metaphoric ingredients of perception and theory which, inevitably in the life of the mind, displace and transform belief and systematic opinion. The composition theory of experience and the vision of a universe of poetry are the source and product of the aesthetic epistemology Shelley expresses in the *Defence.* They seem to have been born from his earlier philosophical position, which regarded "the world and the mind of man as one great whole," when he added the idea that imagination creates from relations between impressions metaphors which integrate and unify thought and existence.

Elsewhere in *Speculations on Metaphysics,* in a passage reflecting his debt to the associationist empiricism of Hartley and Godwin, Shelley speculates suggestively on the possibility of constructing a scale of impressions which, in the tradition of Hume, would be the perfect empiricist cosmology. The passage describes very well the relational concept of experience upon which he based his matrix (or field) theory of consciousness in the *Defence.*

> A scale might be formed, graduated according to the degrees of a combined ratio of intensity, duration, connection, periods of recurrence and utility which would be the standard according to which all ideas might be measured and an uninterrupted chain of nicely shadowed distinctions would be observed, from the faintest impression on the senses to the most distinct combination of those impressions; from the simplest of those combinations to that mass of knowldege which, including our own nature, constitute what we call the universe. (*SM,* VII, 60)

In terms of Shelley's development this statement looks backward to his utilitarian empiricism rather than forward to his myth of metaphor, but it indicates nonetheless his distinctive sensitivity to activity in conceptual space and to transformations among the objects of thought, and thus it reflects the elements of the universe of poetry he later conceived. It can serve as a measure of the philosophic power of his mind to suggest that Plato's analysis of experience connects with that of Berkeley and Hume at just the point Shelley expresses here: the ingredients of experience reflect the structure of opinion, not the structure of reality. Presumably the faintest impression, simply considered, would include the whole field of sensation and impulse, including all elements of rare and aberrant experience. The next level or degree of organization would include such comparatively stable entities of common experience as colors, headaches, trees, houses, and people. Probably it would also include such things as indeterminate experiments and theorems—what Shelley calls our "habits of civil and religious action," and other forms and fruit of human opinion. The next area would probably include all the more stable relational apprehensions of the mind which make up permanent qualities in poetry and other works of art, theories, and systems of principles regulating action.

A general resemblance between this scheme and the Platonic classification of the objects of human knowledge in the *Republic* and in the *Symposium* (which Shelley translated in 1818) is evident: from Plato on, the hierarchic pattern is archetypal in the discourse of western civilization. The most significant difference between Plato's scheme and the version of it prepared for Shelley by Berkeley and Hume is ontological. Plato's dialogues are often enough dramatic representations of attempts to elicit dialectically a principle of correspondence between the ultimate forms and the mind's fundamental ideas. Shelley's conception of the Intellectual Philosophy employs a principle of coherence-for-the-mind as an ontological criterion. This position is clearly expressed, often in phrases taken bodily into the *Defence,*

in his essay *On Life;* their citation here will help to clarify the partial and rich congruence between platonic
and empirical epistemology exploited in the *Defence*
and to show more fully the concept of mind and the
theory of experience it employs.

> It is a decision against which all persuasions struggle,
> and we must be long convicted before we can be con-
> vinced that the solid universe of external things is "such
> stuff as dreams are made of". . . . Whatever may be
> [man's] true and final destination, there is a spirit within
> him at enmity with nothingness and dissolution. This is
> the character of all life and being. Each is at once the
> center and the circumference, the point to which all
> things are referred and the line in which all are con-
> tained. (*OL*, VII, 194)

At the center, genetically speaking, are impressions; at
the circumference, as we shall see, are mythopoeic principles of the world for each mind: "The view of life presented by the most refined deductions of the intellectual
philosophy is that of unity. Nothing exists but as it is
perceived" (*OL*, VI, 196).

At the conclusion of the essay *On Life* is a passage
which appears to have gone unnoticed by those who
have written on *Adonais* but which conducts us very
surely into the argument and conclusion of that poem
as well as to the *Defence* and helps to establish the unity
and direction of Shelley's thought in this later period.

> Let it not be supposed that this doctrine [that nothing
> exists but as it is perceived] conducts to the monstrous
> presumption that I, the person who now writes and
> thinks, am that one mind. *I* am but a portion of it. The
> words *I* and *you* and *they* are grammatical devices in-
> vented simply for arrangement, and totally devoid of
> the intense and exclusive sense usually attached to
> them. It is difficult to find terms adequate to express so

> subtle a conception as that to which the Intellectual Phi-
> losophy has conducted us. We are on that verge where
> words abandon us, and what wonder if we grow dizzy to
> look down the dark abyss of how little we know. (*OL,*
> VI, 196)

The self, others; the mind, the world; truth, error—all
the distinctions and categories of the world system and
its universe of discourse are suspended from their privi-
leged reality in our mental habits as one begins to think
through the implications of the Intellectual Philosophy.
What resulted for Shelley was a new conviction of the
power of imagination and a fresh sense of the role of the
elements of experience as materials of poetry. In the
next passage we have the first clear indication of the
position that was to develop in the *Defence* into the
idea that experience itself is a composition in a universe
of poetry.

> The relations of things remain unchanged by whatever
> system. By the word things is to be understood any ob-
> ject of thought—that is any thought upon which other
> thought is employed with an apprehension of distinc-
> tion. The relations of these remain unchanged; and
> such is the material of our knowledge. (*OL,* VI, 196)

The theory of relational and metaphoric apprehension is built on these foundations: imagination establishes and expresses the relations between "the materials
of knowledge, power, and pleasure" (*D,* VII, 134). Its
integrative and organizing power is a positive (and the
only significant) indication of the mind's unity. (That
nothing can be known to exist independently of mind is
only a negative indication of its unity, as Hume had
shown.) In the only meaningful sense that has remained
epistemologically, the mind is that unity which it creates
among the myriad relations and distinctions it appre-
hends. Metaphor therefore is more an act of transcen-

dence than a manifestation of a transcendent reality, as Sidney had suggested, for example, in *An Apology for Poetry*. By creatively organizing consciousness, metaphor keeps the mind in touch with the basic conditions of being and knowing, rather than serving only to bring forth the dark archetypal realities of a world inaccessible to consciousness. As the mind becomes aware of its contribution to what it takes or has taken for objective reality, it becomes immediately aware also of the constructive and transformational power of metaphor and of the distinct antithetical or complementary activity of reason. Poetry, in Shelley's general sense, does not enlarge "the circumference of the mind" in a simple additive manner, heaping novelty on novelty; it achieves this end chiefly, in all areas of human activity, by the progressive modification, considered earlier as metamorphosis and transfiguration, of the systems of relations usually taken for reality.

To see how Shelley describes the emergence of principles of reality for the imagination, we must return to his use of the circle and related metaphors in the *Defence* and the later poetry. We have seen already that a metaphor is essentially an integral thought made by the mind in the same manner as imagination acts on the material of immediate awareness "so as to color them with its own light, and composing from them as from elements, other thoughts, each containing within itself the principle of its own integrity." What can now be established in interpreting Shelley's metaphoric picture of imagination as the total field of human apprehension is that the circle represents a dynamic system which develops outward from the center. A passage near the end of the *Defence* expresses more fully the directional character of metaphoric transformations within the field of imagination than does the earlier passage on the expansion of its circumference.

> Poetry is indeed something divine. It is at once the cen-
> ter and circumference of knowledge; it is that which
> comprehends all science and that to which all science
> must be referred. It is at the same time the root and
> blossom of all other systems of thought. (*D,* VI, 135)

All systems of thought arise as metaphor in Shelley's
sense. The relations of thoughts synthesized by imagination in immediate experience transform the whole field
of thought and action as they develop and terminate in
the great metaphors and myths of individual and cultural life. Figuratively, the root is at the center, the blos-
som is at the circumference, and the movement from
center to circumference proceeds in accordance with
"the permanent analogy of things" to enlarge the whole
field of imagination. This permanent analogy of things
constitutes a kind of archetypal pattern which directs
the transformational process as "thoughts of ever new
delight" appear in metaphoric apprehension and expression and spread across the field of imagination, as-
similating old thoughts to their new life and creating by
displacement voids in the network of feeling and belief
which call then for new acts of imagination.

In saying that poetry is "that which comprehends all
science and that to which all science must be referred,"
Shelley does not mean natural science alone but all human knowledge—the entire quasi-system of human belief, policy, and theory with its characteristic western
structure: from grand inclusive basic truth—the symbols, standards, and axioms enthroned to regulate life
and thought—down to the most particular beliefs, propositions, and impressions. Architectural metaphors and
metaphors of ascent from experience to theory and de-
scent from theory to experience constitute a closely-
determined, standardized model for western accounts of
the hierarchical structure of human knowledge and
other institutions; and within this system of explication,

univocal propositions represent the building blocks by which the universe of discourse is made to correspond to the reigning world system. Shelley's figure of the circle of imagination is a rival of the architectural model, as his concept of metaphor is a rival of the notion that the univocal proposition is the basic unit of significant mental activity.

The concept of mind which supports his coherence theory of truth or reality for the mind has already been considered; more evidence of the transformations of imaginative experience appears when he indicates how science itself derives from imagination.

> The whole objection, however, of the immorality of poetry rests on a misconception of the manner in which poetry acts to produce the moral improvement of man. Ethical science arranges the elements which poetry has created, and propounds schemes and examples of civil and domestic life. (*D*, VII, 117)

These elements, as we have seen, are metaphoric, and each contains "within itself the principle of its own integrity." It is presumably after the metaphors created by imagination have developed the power to transform habit and custom that the various cultural technologists set about arranging the means and ends of human activity along utilitarian lines. As this arrangement and systematization goes on the "integral thoughts" delivered in the metaphors of poets gradually become, as indicated earlier, "signs for portions and classes of thoughts," lose their integrity for the mind, and finally become subjected to the logic of the cultural system they first brought to life.

> At length the ancient system of religion and manners had fulfilled the circle of its revolutions. And the world would have fallen into utter anarchy and darkness, but that there were found poets among the authors of the

Christian and chivalric systems of manners and religion,
who created forms of opinion and action never before
conceived; which, copied into the imaginations of men,
became as generals to the bewildered armies of their
thoughts. (*D*, VII, 125)

Shelley's focus is not and need not be on historical cau-
sality; it is, rather, squarely on the thesis that history is
mind made in at least two senses: mind creates the elements of solutions to human problems and mind composes the story or poem of their resolution.

The modes, institutions, and principles of conduct
with which ethical science begins, like the elements of
all other science, are poetry in Shelley's general sense of
creations of the human imagination. The definition of
reason as "the enumeration of quantities already
known" appears in many forms in his argument—
always to enforce his conviction of the priority of imagination. The arguments and terminology of his earlier
prose and of the *Defence* show that he was thoroughly
familiar with the instrumental and quantitative bias of
the empirical and utilitarian positions. For example,
Godwin and others had gone far towards the view that
in relation to such notions as self-interest, desire, and
opinion, the notions of virtue, love, and knowledge represent merely second-order abstractions which are codified by verbal signs and syntactically regulated in usage.
They are cultural fictions which have their use in regulating human attitudes but are void of significance as elements of ontology or descriptive psychology.

Against this general position, which constituted the
philosophic backdrop of Thomas Love Peacock's la-
conic *Four Ages of Poetry*, Shelley held that it is from
poetry alone that society obtains its ideas and idealisms
of love, truth, beauty, virtue, and pleasure; they are real
for the mind but cannot be accounted for by the objec-
tivist principles of the Reason-Nature system of the

world. And thus he looks to imagination and within the scope of its operation to metaphoric apprehension and expression for the source of "the value of those quantities, both separately and as a whole," which are distributed by the "calculating processes" of reason (*D*, VII, 135).

A rejected version of the opening lines of the *Defence* indicates fairly graphically the career of his philosophic thought, and also reveals the force of the whole line of its argument. Doubtless the following passage was set aside partly because, rhetorically speaking, it leans too heavily on evanescent philosophic issues "to please many and please long," and, more significantly, because it slides by the concept Shelley sought of the active, integrative function of imagination. This is the central idea of the final version and in its relation to the concepts of metaphor and *poesis* it is the cornerstone of Shelley's position. The opening and closing observations are most important.

> In one mode of considering these two classes of the human mind which are called reason and imagination, the former may be considered as mind employed upon the relations borne by one thought to another, however produced, and imagination is mind combining the elements of thought itself. It has been termed the power of association; and on an accurate anatomy of the functions of the mind, it would be difficult to assign any other origin to the mass of what we perceive and know than this power. Association is, however, rather a law according to which this power is exerted than the power itself; in the same manner as gravitation is a passive expression of the reciprocal tendency of heavy bodies towards their respective centers. Were these bodies conscious of such a tendency, the name which they would assign to that consciousness would express the cause of gravitation; and it were a vain inquiry as to what might be the cause of that cause. Association

> bears the same relation to imagination as a mode to a
> source of action: when we look upon shapes in the fire
> or the clouds and imagine to ourselves the resemblance
> of familiar objects, we do more than seize the relation of
> certain points of visible objects, and fill up, blend to-
> gether. . . .[24]

In this version, imagination is the source of association,
but it is a source only of permutations of given elements—like Coleridge's notion of the fancy. It is not yet
the synthetic agent of integral relations he sought and
found in the concept of metaphor as primary poesis. As
far as it goes the logic of the passage seems to be this: if
imagination combines the *elements* of thought and if,
because all things exist as they are perceived, thoughts
and things are equivalent, then imagination is the
source of the world—an endless, kaleidoscopic array of
meaninglessly associated thing-thoughts. What is miss-
ing here and what is crucial in the final mythopoeic vision of culture is the notion that the elements of thought
as combined by imagination are integral relations (VII,
109) related as the elements of metaphor are; by their
semeiotic adequacy to relational apprehensions which
are not present for the mind in any of the familiar elements of experience. In the final version, with the addi-
tion of this idea of metaphor, Shelley's argument makes
imagination the source of integrations which construe
the world and make it possible for man to distinguish
himself from things-in-permutation.

To use one of the phrases Coleridge had applied to a
problem after undergoing a similar conversion from ne-
cessitarianism to liberation, the mind is still too much a
"lazy-looker-on" in Shelley's rejected version: the
source of a world which fails to signify. In the final form
imagination is portrayed as the active source of all sig-

24 See John Jordan, *A Defence of Poetry and The Four Ages
of Poetry* (New York, 1965), p. 25.

nificance. The germ of this idea is pretty clearly present in the closing account of how elements of thought apprehended as a bare framework are *filled-in* by imagination. With the concept of metaphor added we can see how he thought imagination transforms these elements into signifying relations. (This is perhaps the closest approach Shelley could have made to Berkeley's idea that sensation is the language of the Author of nature and that man construes his world by learning to read this language.) Of his final position on the idea of relational apprehension more will be said later.

The closing phrases of the rejected passage are a precise, if unfortunately brief, phenomenological description of the process of imaginative integration of relations central in the later accounts of imagination and metaphor. However adequate it may be as a philosophic account of the relations of sense data to perception, this passage is an excellent statement of what the mind does and can do with the furniture of ordinary experience in a cultural tradition. And it suggests again the close relationship between Shelley's and Plato's conceptions of the mind's place in culture. Man's values and purposes and instruments arise from such metaphor- and myth-making processes and live only as long as that awareness lasts.

But Shelley's main argument, like Sidney's, goes beyond the question of the place of the products of poetry among the institutions or works of human culture. "Poetry acts in another and diviner manner" than by providing the elements of man's cultural environment: it informs and in a sense creates the spirit in man from which his cultural life develops. He receives directly from culture (as from a reflection of his own inner being) motives to personal and social creativity and knowledge of the potentialities of his own nature. Love, for example, is seen as an imaginative action of the human spirit in which the basic laws of the cultural process are reflected:

> The great secret of morals is love; or a going out of our
> own nature, and an identification of ourselves with the
> beautiful which exists in thought, action or person not
> our own. . . . The great instrument of moral good is im-
> agination; and poetry administers to the effect by acting
> on the cause. (*D*, VII, 118)

As described in this passage empathy itself is a kind of
existential metaphor—not feeling *for* but feeling *as* another is a possibility of self-transcendence which reflects
in social life the universal principle by which the mind is
awakened to immediate awareness of the conditions of
its own activity. Shelley in his account of the genesis of
social sympathy distinguishes carefully, though implic-
itly, between the elements of experience envisioned by
rationalist utilitarians and those intelligible in terms of
his own idealism of imagination:

> The social sympathies, or those laws from which, as
> from its elements, society results, begin to develop
> themselves from the moment that two human beings
> coexist; the future is contained within the present, as
> the plant within the seed; and equality, diversity, unity,
> contrast, mutual dependence, become the principles
> alone capable of affording the motives according to
> which the will of a social being is determined to action,
> inasmuch as he is social; and constitute pleasure in sen-
> sation, virtue in sentiment, beauty in art, truth in rea-
> soning, and love in the intercourse of kind. (*D*,VII, 110)

The relations here called principles are not
sensations but what Locke had called "ideas of reflection." They are mental principles which name relations
between thoughts of imagination or ideas of sensation.
Sensation can afford the motives according to which a
person can be determined to action inasmuch as he is

animal; but the mental principles Shelley identifies are principles of the synthetic activity of imagination by which the mind itself creates, in accordance with the permanent analogies among its thoughts, the modes of experience he calls pleasure, virtue, beauty, truth, and love. The mind's capacity for relational, metaphoric apprehension produces these and all generative ideas and ideals and thus constitutes the cultural "dome of many-colored glass [which] stains the white radiance of eternity." [25] The dome is inevitably a fabric of metaphor. Given Shelley's conception of the Intellectual Philosophy, its elements cannot be reduced as the empiricists and utilitarians urged to names for associated sensations because *poesis* is primitive for the mind and not the "unbelievable" abstractions of atomic sensations or primary qualities. [26] When the continuation of his passage on "ethical science" is considered more fully it can be better understood how from the metaphoric process the dynamic field of man's mind and culture develops through the expansion of imagination.

> But poetry acts in another and diviner manner. It awakens and enlarges the mind itself by rendering it the receptacle of a thousand unapprehended combinations of thought. Poetry lifts the veil from the hidden beauty of the world, and makes familiar objects be as if they were not familiar. . . . (*D*, VII, 117)

The quasi-platonic image of the receptacle used here is another of the spatial metaphors which pictures the structure of the process of metaphoric transformation. If we recall that (1) everything exists as it is perceived, at least in relation to the percipient, (2) imagination is

[25] Shelley, *Adonais*, II, 404. He wrote "life . . . stains the white radiance of eternity," but it is correct, I believe, to qualify it here as cultural life.

[26] Alfred North Whitehead, *Science in the Modern World* (New York, 1925), pp. 49-57.

mind composing from its thoughts other thoughts, each containing within itself the principle of its own integrity, and (3) metaphor is the apprehension and expression of these integral relations of thought to thought, it becomes clearer that poetry, as the principle of synthesis, fills and expands the field of consciousness with a thousand combinations of thought unapprehended by the reason-sense mode of experience—and that these metaphors are more integral and intelligible for the mind, which has thus made them, than the arbitrary associations of sense and the conventional operations of reason can be. It is by means of synthetic apprehension that the mind "creates anew the universe [of poetry] after it has been annihilated in our minds by the recurrence of impressions [including, surely, sensations, beliefs, and ideas] blunted by reiteration" (*D*, VII, 137). Shelley's metaphors of the wind-stream; youth, spring, and morning; the radiance of flower, song, and star; and many others illustrate creative integrations among previously unapprehended relations. Pleasure, virtue, beauty, truth, and love similarly exist for the mind as metaphors; but as grand metaphors it would seem, which emerge from other more immediate apprehensions. Their "high" position in the traditional cosmology of culture is conserved in Shelley's universe of poetry, where they represent "forms" of apprehension in which the various transformations of immediate relational apprehension participate. He is not explicit about the place of these "forms" in the universe of poetry, but their role can be discerned if we return at this point to the question of metaphoric apprehension and see it in relation to his picture of consciousness as a field.

Early in the *Defence* it is established that "to be a poet is to apprehend the true and the beautiful—in a word the good, which exists in the relation, subsisting, first between existence and perception, and secondly between perception and expression" (*D*, VII, 111-112).

In accordance with the principle that "all things exist as
they are perceived" this difficult passage implies simply
that whereas unimaginative experience acquiesces in ha-
bitual and stereotyped modes of apprehension (as in the
case of treating dead metaphors as having reference to
extra-mental realities),[27] imaginative poetic experience,
on the other hand, attends in the spirit of metaphor to
the relational features of immediate experience. To put
it differently, the poet attends to existence on the one
hand in the sense of what he ought to know or feel or
what he believes and expects, and on the other to what
he properly perceives. He attends especially to the inter-
play of these two modes of apprehension. Shelley's own
capacity for this kind of experience is evident everywhere in his poetry and prose. As discrepancies and in-
congruities appear between the two systems of relations,
or as before-unapprehended relations are discerned between any two or more thoughts, the mind may respond
by reducing the novel elements of perception to the familiar forms of existence or by "realizing" as metaphor
the relations thus apprehended. Shelley's reference to
the "true and the beautiful, in a word the good, which
exists in the relation subsisting between existence and
perception . . . " has a platonic appearance. But when
the process he is describing is made more concrete it appears equally possible that he means simply that the
metaphors which

imagination does realize from the relations it appre-
hends in immediate experience have truth and beauty

[27] The critiques by Whitehead of "the fallacy of simple loca-
tion" (*Science and the Modern World*, pp. 53-59), by Richards
of the "proper meaning superstition" (*The Philosophy of Rhetoric*, pp. 73 and 5-12), and by Turbayne of dogmas of categorical
heterogeneity (*The Myth of Metaphor*, pp. 17-18) represent as-
saults from varied perspectives on a citadel of world-system assumptions for which Shelley's *Defence of Poetry* was indeed
"the trumpet of a prophecy."

and are good for the mind because the mind fulfills its expressive and constructive power through them. (Again Shelley is working out a theory of immanent realization within the framework of the Intellectual Philosophy but in terms of transcendental participation: platonism, where conformable, colors the necessary empiricism.)

The motive of such metaphoric apprehension is simply to make something from before-unapprehended relations of things. Madness and alienation appear to be the risks of the process, as Shelley knew; learning and freedom are its benefits, as is poetry. Like John Keats in *Adonais* and Emilia Viviani in *Epipsychidion,* the mythical Prometheus undergoes a profound transfiguration in the metaphoric synthesis of mental imagery in *Prometheus Unbound.* The existent thing, the mythological figure of the civilizing hero with which Shelley's imagination began, is used as the vehicle for his expression of previously-unapprehended relations between the mythic figure and the creative principles of human nature: love and imagination. The poem is programmatic for the theory of the *Defence,* and it illustrates perfectly how mythology like all other human experience is through metaphor transfigured into myth.[28]

[28] Shelley's "Preface" to *Prometheus Unbound* sets forth some of the basic principles and beliefs, and his poem illustrates very richly the ideas of metaphor and the dynamic space of imagination which he spelled out later in the *Defence.* The relationships between these and other works of the later period require a separate study. In describing the imagery of *Prometheus Unbound,* Shelley indicates (but does not name as metaphor) the kinds of relational apprehension central in the argument of the *Defence:* "the imagery which I have employed will be found, in many instances, to have been drawn from the operations of the human mind, or from those external actions by which they are expressed" (II, 172). Wasserman's excellent discussion of the structure and imagery of the poem does not make use of Shelley's conception of metaphor and mythmaking: See *Shelley's Prometheus Unbound,* pp. 54-57.

If we return to Shelley's circle figure, it can now be shown more fully that metaphoric apprehension is the genesis and that mythic ideality is the *telos* of the transformations which constitute experience in the universe of poetry. The center of the field of imagination is immediate experience, and it consists in the proper apprehensions of the individual. Its central activity is apprehension of "thoughts" and of the relations between them. Through this process what is immediately evident for the individual in sensation, thought, or emotion is seen as relations of things before not apprehended: transcendence is initiated, and learning and the other higher activities of the human spirit emerge—knowing beyond opinion, benevolence beyond self-interest, and love beyond desire. The metaphors produced by the immediate synthetic activity of imagination are "new materials of knowledge and power, and pleasure" (*D,* VII, 134). After their realization, at the center of experience, these apprehensions develop and displace dead and inadequate systems of belief and forms of action, and they transform existing relations in the mind or culture until the circumference of imagination itself is expanded and the metaphor has been transformed into myth. Experience or the world for the mind is therefore a composition, a version of the "great poem"[29] which has life, and which grows through man's aware-

[29] When Shelley refers to the "great poem" he does not pause to remind the reader of the sense in which all men are poets or that all language is poetry: "In the infancy of society [in any of its revolutions] every author is necessarily a poet, because language itself is poetry" (*D,* VII, 111). He merely observes in passing that particular poems should be regarded "as episodes to that great poem which all poets, like the cooperating thoughts of one great mind, have built up since the beginning of the world" (*D,* VII, 124). His emphasis is on the cosmic drama of human culture in which the human mind composes the universe of poetry. The essence of "the one mind" is the one activity of imaginative metamorphosis: the sonnet of a moment or the world poem of an age participate in this process.

ness of the relations of things real for his mind, and which receives its expression in the works and actions of his cultural life. From each single metaphor the world poem exfoliates by metamorphosis into myth.

> Thought
> Alone, and its quick elements, Will, Passion,
> Reason, imagination, cannot die;
> They are what that which they regard appears,
> The stuff whence mutability can weave
> All that it hath dominion o'er,—worlds, worms,
> Empires, and superstitions. [30]

---

[30] *Hellas*, II, p. 44, ll. 795-801.

IV

ADONAIS illustrates and illuminates the *Defence* far more completely than has been supposed. In two crucial respects it confirms the position we have been studying: (1) dramatically it enacts the epistemological principle of seeing reality-for-man as metaphor and myth made by imagination, and (2) it deliberately converts mythology into myth in accordance with the principle that vital metaphor (and myth) must contain "within itself the principle of its own integrity." A brief examination of the conclusion of the elegy will make both of these points clear and serve to confirm the general argument of this essay. It will be desirable first, however, to indicate some of the relevant conclusions of Earl Wasserman's study of *Adonais* and to suggest how the account to follow here relates to his important discoveries about the poem's genre and mode, to the inner structure of its imagery and its movement, and to the conception of Shelley's mythmaking which he developed later in *Shelley's Prometheus Unbound.*

Wasserman regards *Adonais* as a three-part composition whose concluding movement of assurance (traditional in the pastoral elegy) that death is somehow overcome and grief legitimately abandoned evolves "organically" from materials fully present initially but not then understood.[31] The poem's progress constitutes a kind of dramatic lesson in philosophic idealism prearranged for the elegist by Shelley. "The ultimate revelation of the elegy, therefore, has been present from the beginning, and the forward drive through the three acts of the drama resides in the urgency with which the ele-

[31] *The Subtler Language,* p. 320.

ments of the poem need to press upon their observer the full and proper meaning they contain."[32]

Awareness of the poem's dramatic character and the latent elements of its vision is crucial. Its value is obscured, however, by an account of the perfected and liberating "revelation" of the final movement as a recognition by the elegist that "Although the Many change and pass, the One remains. Here in the symbol-charged cemetery [at Rome, stanzas XLVIII-LII] the mourner can *see* why he should mourn no longer."[33] Throughout the analysis the critic supposes that Shelley knows or believes in this perfecting intuition of transcendental participation. The unfortunate tendency of this supposition to a kind of supernaturalist literalism is evident when he explains what it is that the elegist is made to "see" and in turn relate to the "fond wretch" (whom Wasserman, wrongly, I think, believes is the reader or some other and not the elegist as well): "the mourner will know himself aright when he knows that even in the mortal world his essential reality is a star-soul that can reach beyond the false mutability of 'our day and night.'" [34] A convincing demonstration of the great importance of these systems of images in the composition is flawed by a frame of reference which converts the metaphors of Shelley's dramatic myth into symbols significant not immediately as integral relations but discursively within a platonic ontology of the type Wasserman's valuable analysis is designed to displace.[35] The mythopoetic design of *Adonais* should be sought first in Shelley's own extraordinary accounts of metaphor- and myth-making in the *Defence*.

Again in relation to the *Defence*, Wasserman's account of Shelley's myth-making in *Prometheus Un-*

[32] Ibid., p. 361.
[33] Ibid., p. 350.
[34] Ibid., p. 346.
[35] Cf. ibid., pp. 312-313, 343-348.

bound appears to miss what Shelley came to believe about poesis. The following statement, for example, contains important truth and yet is misleading about his notion of myth-making: "Shelley conceives of the poet as not merely an assimilator of beautiful mythic forms: inasmuch as he is creative, he is a mythopoeist, not by inventing myths, but by reconstituting the imperfect ones that already exist."[36] When Shelley's conception of metaphor is rightly understood it becomes clear that the "imperfect" myths referred to are not, as this passage suggests, imperfect earlier approximations to truth or great poetry but simply the great (and so far real) myths of the past whose once-living relations have been exhausted by use. Their archetypal elements await imaginative restoration of the kind envisioned in Shelley's own accounts of metaphor and myth.

> A great poem is a fountain forever overflowing with the waters of wisdom and delight; and after one person and one age has exhausted all its divine effluence which their peculiar relations enable them to share, another and another succeeds, and new relations are ever developed, the source of an unforseen and an unconceived delight. (*D*, VII, 131)

Another problematic area where Wasserman has taught us much about how to read Shelley properly is that of the genre of his poetry.

> I have chosen to examine the poetry of Shelley because I believe our failure to find coherent meaning in it and the resulting conspicuous comtempt in which it is held by modern critics are the result of a failure to recognise that it is internally constitutive not only of its own reality, but also of the vocabulary and syntax of that reality. We have customarily come to it with assumptions of a relational system other than its own and have protested

[36] *Shelley's Prometheus Unbound*, p. 68.

that it refuses to behave according to our laws. . . .[37]

Traditional conceptions of genre and the mimetic theory of literature both did long blind critics to the nature of Shelley's poetic achievement. By studying closely the internal and external

. relations of the imagery and other thematic material in *Adonais* and *Prometheus Unbound,* Wasserman has shown concretely not only how these great poems transcend the systems of thought and feeling which some of their materials presented to Shelley, but how also their formal or generic originality may be seen as integral to his vision.

> To these intricate elegiac conventions Shelley adhered with remarkable precision, even to the point of borrowing images, actions and rhetorical patterns from Bion and Moschus. Nevertheless, the translation of Keats into legendary Adonis and the casting of the materials into the traditional elegiac form merely provided Shelley with a way of conceiving his subject and giving it an outward shape. . . . Moreover, the legend and the conventions clearly do not constitute a total control for both are largely terminated by stanza 40.[38]

This well-demonstrated conclusion can now be taken for granted in studying *Adonais,* but not, as I will later explain more fully, a more general conclusion Wasserman draws from it. Of the interrelations of the (metaphoric) imagery in which Shelley united the texture and the dramatic structure of *Adonais* he observes:

> These interrelations of imagistic systems do not constitute the artistry of the elegy any more than does Shelley's strict adherence to the traditional elegiac patterns;

[37] *The Subtler Language,* p. 188.
[38] Ibid., p. 310.

nor indeed are they explicit. Rather they are assumed as pre-existing interconnections in whose texture Shelley shapes his materials to make his artistic statement. [39]

Almost the reverse of this is true as Shelley's account of metaphor should suggest:

> It marks the before unapprehended relations of things and perpetuates their apprehension, until the words which represent them become, through time, signs for portions or classes of thoughts instead of integral thoughts; and then if no new poets should arise to create afresh the associations which have thus been disorganized, language will be dead to all the nobler purposes of human intercourse. (*D,* VII, 111)

The first part of this statement accurately represents the decadent condition of classical and of Christian mythology as perceived by Shelley; the second part beautifully describes what he did with those dead "signs for portions or classes of thought." In ascribing a poetic "statement" to *Adonais* and Shelley, Wasserman's argument seems to throw away some of its best results. Whether this is due to the assumption that *Adonais* relates Shelley's "explicit, and true, answer" to the question, "What is the ultimate reality,"[40] or to other reasons, need not concern us here. The fact remains that Wasserman misses seeing how in Shelley's greatest poems he followed closely his own profound conception of mythmaking: a conception which improved on anything which had preceded it because as we have seen he had sensed in metaphor a key to poesis.

The dramatic cosmology of *Adonais,* through stanza XLVI, is a mixture of elegiac conventions and mythology, animated primarily by Shelley's distinctive genius for mental imagery, the idioms and imagery of neo-

[39] Ibid., p. 326.
[40] Ibid., p. 318.

platonic literature and metaphysics, and the local color of English romanticism. As a philosophic vision it shows what is possible, rather than what is necessary. In the concluding stanzas, however, the elegist confronts his own immediate experience as metaphor and initiates an experience of imaginative transcendence which goes beyond the mythologically possible to a mythopoeic vision of what is actual for his awakened mind. This movement enacts the myth of metaphor in accordance with the philosophic script provided by the *Defence.* The center-circumference figure and its related images are explicit and pivotal. The dramatic action develops as a passage from the center to the circumference of experience in which the division between life and death, self and other, the one and the many is overcome. *Adonais* ends, naturally enough, at the threshold of that experience but its design and significance are unmistakable once the poem's relationship to the *Defence* is understood.

The apparently neo-platonic nature myth, developed gradually through stanza XLVI, is mythology and not living myth for the whole poem. In Stanza XLII the elegist ascends to the thought that Keats "is made one with nature" (XLII). But neo-platonic nature itself is undergoing an imaginative metamorphosis in the spirit of Shelley's myth of metaphor.

> He is a portion of the loveliness
> Which once he made more lovely: he doth bear
> His part, while the one Spirit's plastic stress
> Sweeps through the dull dense world, compelling there
> All new successions to the forms they wear;
> Torturing th' unwilling dross that checks its flight
> To its own likeness, as each mass may bear;
> And bursting in its beauty and its might
> From trees and beasts and men into the Heaven's light.
>   (XLIII)

According to the argument of the *Defence* and Shelley's other philosophic prose of the later period, "the one Spirit's plastic stress" works not—as neo-platonism has it, on substance or matter—but in perception through the agency of imagination. (The Demiurge is to be equated with human imagination.[41]) Accordingly this stanza can be interpreted allegorically as an anticipation of a higher vision the elegist has not yet reached, so long as we remain aware that vision is not instruction.

The "form" Keats has "succeeded" to is revealed as the evening star when the mythological process of the poem reaches its conclusion in stanzas XLV and XLVI, but the principle of integrity, the reason for this metaphoric form of his transfiguration, is not expressed in a manner necessary for the imagination of the elegist and reader until later, in the final two stanzas, LIV and LV.

> The inheritors of unfulfilled renown
> Rose from their thrones, built beyond mortal thought,
> Far in the Unapparent. . . . (XLV)

> "Thou art become as one of us," they cry,
> "It was for thee yon kingless sphere has long
> "Swung blind in unascended majesty,
> "Silent alone amid an Heaven of Song.
> "Assume thy wingèd throne, thou Vesper of our throng!" (XLVI)

This mythological heaven which is part of the circumference of the elegist's imagination at this point in the poem gives way in the following stanza. He turns to confront directly the reader's and his own recalcitrant grief—reinforced as it had doubtless been by the remoteness of the figure of the evening star—and perhaps too by the artificiality of some of the conventional elegiac scenes. He challenges the mourner to transcend his

[41] Cf. R.G. Woodman, *The Apocalyptic Vision in the Poetry of Shelley* (Toronto, 1964), pp. 19-21.

egocentric system of the world.

> Who mourns for Adonais? Oh, come forth,
> Fond wretch! And know thyself and him aright.
> Clasp with thy panting soul the pendulous Earth;
> As from a center dart thy spirit's light
> Beyond all worlds, until its spacious might
> Satiate the void circumference: then shrink
> Even to a point within our day and night;
> And keep thy heart light lest it make thee sink
> When hope has kindled hope, and lured thee to the
>   brink. (XLVII)

As in the *Defence* the circumference of imagination and the circumference of the world for the mind are identified and pictured as craving the creative power of the spirit's light.

> Poetry enlarges the circumference of imagination by re-
> plenishing it with thoughts of ever new delight, which
> have the power of attracting and assimilating to their
> own nature all other thoughts, and which form new in-
> tervals and interstices whose void forever craves fresh
> food. (*D*, VII, 118)

The web image of this passage signifies, as we have seen, a radiating network of relations which make up the world for the mind; and it appears in the same context in *Adonais* where, too weak with grief to dart spontaneously their spirit's light past all known worlds, the elegist and reader go to the metaphorical center of this world—Rome. Rome is a monumental catachresis: "at once the Paradise, / The grave, the city, and the wilderness" (XLIX). It is aglut with metaphor, with before unapprehended relations of things mutable and immutable which put the elegist's imagination in flight (stanzas XLVIII-LI) and lead him to an immediate and mythopoeic experience of the metaphoric relations he had before been fashioning into elegiac mythology.

Once he begins to experience imaginatively the world his imagination has created, his spirit gains strength for its release from crucifixion on the antitheses of time and eternity, the many and the One:

> The One remains, the many change and pass;
> Heaven's light forever shines, Earth's shadows fly;
> Life, like a dome of many-colored glass,
> Stains the white radiance of Eternity,
> Until death tramples it to fragments.—Die,
> If thou wouldst be with that which thou dost seek!
> Follow where all is fled!—Rome's azure sky,
> Flowers, ruins, statues, music, words, are weak
> The glory they transfuse with fitting truth to speak.
> (LII)

Natural existence is renounced again in stanza LIII and then in LIV the imaginative vision is fulfilled as the speaker sees through the web of being which fills man's world from center to circumference:

> That Light whose smile kindles the Universe,
> That Beauty in which all things work and move,
> That Benediction which the eclipsing Curse
> Of birth can quench not, that sustaining Love
> Which through the web of being blindly wove
> By man and beast and earth and air and sea,
> Burns bright or dim, as each are mirrors of
> The fire for which all thirst, now beams on me,
> Consuming the last clouds of cold mortality. (LIV)

The final movement of *Adonais* is an actual event in the imaginative cosmos created by its elegist in accordance with the pattern for a universe of poetry conceived by Shelley in the *Defence.* In both these works the "forms" (Light, Beauty, and Benediction; the True, the Beautiful, and the Good) have the character of dimensions of a cosmic loom (an alternative to space and time) on which as he is directed by imagination or reason, metaphor or custom, man weaves alternately "beautiful idealisms of moral excellence" or great chains of being, presences and poetry or things and institutions. Shelley has substituted a matrix model of human consciousness for traditional images. The motive of his adaptation of the Intellectual Philosophy seems, at least in part, to have been an internalization of the great chain of being as part of treating "the mind of man and the universe as one great whole on which to exercise our speculations" (*SM,* VII, 65).

With the help of his idea that metaphor provides integral "thoughts" for the mind Shelley was able to substitute a theory of learning as a process of symbolic transformation for the neo-platonic vision of an hierarchy of imprisoned yearnings. The web of being is a net or radiant ladder as imagination lives or dies. The elegist in *Adonais* comes to see that men, like all creatures, blindly weave the web of being—a world system in a universe of discourse—until the secret that they weave is found out, as in *Prometheus Unbound.*

Shelley's own progress to this spirit-made and spirit-making vision and its culmination in *Adonais* is strangely charted for us in a passage which reads like an allegory on its own thesis:

> If it were possible that a person should give a faithful history of his being, from the earliest epochs of his recollection, a picture would be presented such as the world has never contemplated before. A mirror would be held up to all men in which they might behold their own recollections, and, in dim perspective, their shadowy hopes and fears,—all that they dare not, or that daring and desiring, they could not expose to the open eyes of day. But thought can with difficulty visit the intricate and winding chambers which it inhabits. It is like a river whose rapid and perpetual stream flows outwards; —like one in dread who speeds through the recesses of some haunted pile, and dares not look behind. The caverns of the mind are obscure, and shadowy; or

pervaded with a lustre, beautifully bright indeed, but
shining not beyond their portals. If it were possible to
be where we have been, vitally and indeed—if, at the
moment of our presence there, we could define the results of our experience,—if the passage from sensation
to reflection—from a state of passive perception to vol-
untary contemplation, were not so dizzying and so tu-
multuous, this attempt would be less difficult. (*SM,* VII,
61)

Prometheus Unbound and *Adonais* are visions of
the mind's break with the so-called real world of habit,
custom, and the fictions of objective nature and finite
selfhood. Immaterialism was the instrument of his de-
scent into these caverns of awakened consciousness and
his account of it clearly follows Bishop Berkeley.

It reduces the mind to that freedom in which it would
have acted, but for the misuse of words and signs, the
instruments of its own creation. By signs, I would be
understood in a wide sense, including what is properly
meant by that term, and what I particularly mean. In
this latter sense, almost all familiar objects are signs,
standing, not for themselves, but for others, in their capacity of suggesting one thought which shall lead to a
train of thoughts. Our whole life is then an education in
error. (*OL,* VI, 195)

His myth of metaphor grew directly from the philosophic radicalism which regards the elements of experience as the "language of the Author of nature."[42] It is-
sued in the essay *On Life* in an account of the dread he
sensed in his release from the "error," and it clearly
forecasted the conclusion of *Adonais.* "We are on that
verge where words abandon us, and what wonder if we

[42] Cf. George Berkeley, *Three Dialogues* in *Works,* II
(London, 1948-1957), p. 183 ff., and C.M. Turbayne, "Editor's
Commentary," in *Works on Vision* (New York, 1963), pp. xxvii-
xxxvii, xli-xlv.

grow dizzy to look down the dark abyss of how little we know" (*OL,* VI, 196). Imagination in poesis is the Author of nature, and in *Adonais* Shelley wrote a reading of its language: the elements of life, before unapprehended relations of things, are integrated as myth.

In these terms the metamorphosis and transfiguration of John Keats into Herperus, "a splendour in the firmament of time," is a transformation of one of the radiant bearers of light, a Luciferian servant of Prometheus, into a source for all time of the only light man will ever have, the light of his own creative activity. The fire which beams on the elegist is this fire of imagination kindled by his own metaphor and myth-making effort—and at last burning away the final strands of his bondage to the literal: ego and death. The final stanza of *Adonais* turns on the same figure of the earth and circumambient heaven which marked the poem's climactic shift from elegaic mythology to mythopoeic vision.

> The breath whose might I have invoked in song
> Descends on me; my spirit's bark is driven,
> Far from the shore, far from the trembling throng
> Whose sails were never to the tempest given;
> The massy earth and sphered skies are riven!
> I am borne darkly, fearfully, afar;
> Whilst, burning through the inmost veil of Heaven,
> The soul of Adonais, like a star,
> Beacons from the abode where the Eternal are. (LV)

Until the elegist had symbolically gone to Rome and fed his imagination on before unapprehended relations of things at the living ruin of the heart of the world—to which proverbially, all roads lead—his spirit was blind and bound in the network of conventional and mythological relations which separate center and circumference. The apparent drift toward death in the concluding section of the poem is initiated by this experience of

transcendence and has two distinct levels of significance: it represents a literal suicidal urge to the ego of
the elegist and to the reader who does not see through
the world system; it is metaphoric and represents an anticipation of the final transcendence of self and the
world system to the liberated imagination. One should
not, I think, try to choose between these interpretations
of the concluding movement; and their relative force
need not be considered here: what is most distinctively
Shelleyan in the episode and what most illuminates his
idea of the role of metaphor in the universe of poetry is
expressed very directly in the *Defence:*

> All things exist as they are perceived; at least in relation
> to the percipient. 'The mind is its own place, and of it-
> self can make a heaven of hell, a hell of heaven.' But po-
> etry defeats the curse which binds us to be subjected to
> the accident of surrounding impressions. And whether it
> spreads its own figured curtain, or withdraws life's dark
> veil from before the scene of things, it equally creates
> for us a being within our being. It makes us inhabitants
> of a world to which the familiar world is a chaos. It re-
> produces the common universe of which we are por-
> tions and percipients, and it purges from our inward
> sight the film of familiarity which obscures from us the
> wonder of our being. It compels us to feel that which we
> perceive, and to imagine that which we know. (*D*, VII,
> 137)

Such feeling and imagination creates and recovers
the poetry, the metaphors and myths with which man
weaves the world he lives in. In *Adonais* the elegist first
spreads a "figured curtain" of conventional mythology,
and then at Rome he finally "withdraws life's dark veil
from before the scene of things," initiating a truly mythopoeic vision of the unity of creative apprehension. The
familiar world becomes a chaos for him—"cold hopes
swarm like worms within our living clay"; but its ele-

ments are transformed and reunited by metaphoric vision and give rise at the end to a myth of communion and transfiguration, "as each are mirrors of the fire for which all thirst," and ego is transcended, bewilderingly, *seeing* and *reflecting* Adonais, Hesper, Keats. Mythology merely possible is transformed by this metaphor of interanimating communion to actual immediate experience which possesses that philosophic necessity provided by Shelley's interpretation of the Intellectual Philosophy and which possesses the self-authenticating quality of living myth. Adonais' soul beacons not as a physical star to the elegist passionately contemplating it; it beacons *"like a star"* to the light-mirroring imagination of the poet who has fashioned the mythopoeic instrument of its reflection.

Just as the elegist finally transcends the world-system literalism which held his ego in bondage to grief and fear of death, the reader is called upon to yield the literal linguistic and cosmological props of ordinary (ordinal) experience and be inducted into the universe of poetry. The line "What Keats is why fear we to become" does not imply a project of dying: it is a call to imaginative awakening, a call to "a myth not to be taken literally, but to be dwelt on . . . till the charm of it touches one deeply—so deeply that when the 'initiated' say 'it is not true,' one is able to answer by acting as if it were true."[43] The polarity of time and eternity, the duality and opposition of center and circumference, is transcended. With his vision of thematic unity among the metaphoric transformations which comprise the web of being for the mind, the elegist becomes the poetry he has made of Keats. Soul mirrors soul: "before unapprehended relations of things" signify the unity of being for imagination in stanza LIV: the mirror and beacon of Keats's soul sends and receives light to the in-

[43] J.A. Stewart, *The Myths of Plato* (London, 1960), p. 132.

tegrated and integrating soul of the poet.

The apotheosis of imagination at the end of *Adonais* leads directly to the universe of poetry pre-conceived in the *Defence*. Like Keats and his elegist, these two works illuminate and illustrate each other in many more ways than have been considered here; but they do so particularly for the cardinal point of each—the vision of the mind as a field filled with evidences in the transfiguration of metaphor into myth of the unity and communion of the human spirit. From the perspective of Shelley's additions to aesthetic epistemology, experience is that circle whose center is wherever metaphor occurs, and whose circumference is everywhere myth. Neither can have any sense without the other—experience can have no unity without both.

> EVERYTHING IS ONLY A METAPHOR;
> THERE IS ONLY POETRY.[44]

---

[44] Norman O. Brown, *Love's Body* (New York, 1968), p. 266.

BIBLIOGRAPHY

Abrams, Meyer H. *The Mirror and the Lamp: Romantic Theory and the Critical Tradition.* New York: W.W. Norton and Co., 1958.

Bachelard, Gaston. *The Poetics of Space,* trans. Maria Jolas. New York: Orion Press, 1964.

———. *The Psychoanalysis of Fire,* trans. Alan C.M. Ross. Boston: Beacon Press, 1964.

Baker, Carlos H. *Shelley's Major Poetry.* New York: Russell and Russell, 1961.

Barfield, Owen. *Poetic Diction.* London: Faber and Faber, 1952.

———. *Saving the Appearances: A Study in Idolatry.* New York: Harcourt, Brace and World, 1957.

Berkeley, George. *Works,* ed. A.A. Luce and T.E. Jessop. Edinburgh: Nelson and Sons, 1948-1957.

———. *Works on Vision,* ed. C.M. Turbayne. New York: Bobbs-Merrill Company, 1962.

Blake, William. *Complete Writings,* ed. Geoffrey Keynes. London: Oxford University Press, 1966.

Bloom, Harold. *Shelley's Mythmaking.* New Haven: Yale University Press, 1959.

Brown, Norman O. *Love's Body.* New York: Random House, 1966.

Coleridge, Samuel Taylor. *The Statesman's Manual.* London: Gale and Fenner, 1816.

Drummond, Sir William. *Academical Questions,* Vol. I. London: W. Boliner and Co., 1805.

Gerard, Albert S. *English Romantic Poetry: Ethos, Structure, and Symbol in Coleridge, Wordsworth, Shelley, and Keats.* Berkeley: University of California Press, 1968.

Goodman, Nelson. *Languages of Art.* New York: Bobbs-Merrill, 1968.

Hesse, Mary B. "The Explanatory Function of Metaphor," in *International Congress for Logic Methodology, and Philosophy of Science,* ed. Y. Bar-Hillel. Amsterdam: North-Holland Publication Company, 1965.

Howell, Wilbur S. *Logic and Rhetoric in England, 1500-1700.* New York: Russell and Russell, 1961.

Hume, David. *A Treatise of Human Nature.* Oxford: Oxford University Press, 1967.

Locke, John. *An Essay Concerning Human Understanding.* Oxford: Oxford University Press, 1924.

Murray, Henry A. "The Possible Nature of a Mythology to Come," in *Myth and Mythmaking,* ed. Henry A. Murray. New York: Beacon Press, 1968.

Newton, Sir Isaac. *Opticks.* New York: Oxford University Press, 1952.

Nicolson, Marjorie H. *The Breaking of the Circle.* New York: Columbia University Press, 1960.

Plato. *The Myths of Plato,* ed. J.A. Stewart. London: Macmillan, 1905.

Poulet, Georges. *Les Métamorphoses du Cèrcle.* Paris: Plon, 1961.

Pulos, C.E. *The Deep Truth.* Lincoln: University of Nebraska Press, 1954.

Quine, Willard V.O. *From A Logical Point of View.* Cambridge: Harvard University Press, 1953.

Richards, Ivor A. *The Philosophy of Rhetoric.* New York: Oxford University Press, 1936.

Schulze, Earl J. *Shelley's Theory of Poetry: A Reappraisal.* The Hague: Mouton Press, 1966.

Shelley, Percy Bysshe. *The Complete Works of Shelley,* ed. Roger Ingpen and W.E. Peck. New York: Gordian Press, 1965.

――――. and Peacock, T.L. *A Defence of Poetry and the Four Ages of Poetry,* ed. John E. Jordan. New York: Bobbs-Merrill Company, 1965.

――――. *The Letters of Percy Bysshe Shelley,* ed. F.L. Jones. Oxford: Oxford University Press, 1964.

Turbayne, Colin M. *The Myth of Metaphor.* New Haven: Yale University Press, 1962.

Wasserman, Earl R. "Shelley's Last Poetics: a Reconsideration," in *From Sensibility to Romanticism: Essays Presented to Frederick A. Pottle,* ed. F.W. Hilles and Harold Bloom. New York: Oxford University Press, 1965.

———. *Shelley's Prometheus Unbound,* Baltimore: John Hopkins Press, 1965.

———. *The Subtler Language.* Baltimore: Johns Hopkins Press, 1959.

Watts, Isaac. *Logick: or the Right Use of Reason in the Enquiry after Truth.* London: Ford and Hett, 1736.

Whitehead, A.N. *Science and the Modern World.* New York: Macmillan, 1925.

Woodings, Robert B. *Shelley: Modern Judgments.* New York: Macmillan, 1968.

Woodman, Ross G. *The Apocalyptic Vision in the Poetry of Shelley.* Toronto: University of Toronto Press, 1964.

Yates, Frances A. *Giordano Bruno and the Hermetic Tradition.* Chicago: University of Chicago Press, 1964.

INDEX

142587